TOP JOCKEY

THE PROFESSIONALS BETTING STRATEGY REVEALED

BRIAN HUGHES – CHARMANT Winning Odds – 21.23

RICHARD KINGSCOTE – INVOLVED Winning Odds 32.0

LUKE MORRIS – I LOVE YOU BABY winning odds 52.97

BEN CURTIS - MANNAABIT 19.5 just a few of our big priced recent winners highlighted by this method

FORWARD

Our scheme to relieve the bookmakers of some of their cash, and had been many months in the planning only to be scuppered by a poor ride by an inexperienced apprentice jockey, since that day we have only placed bets on what we consider to be TOP JOCKEYS, Read on................

A few years ago myself along with a few close and trusted friends who had been involved in a very successful betting syndicate decided to take our interest in the sport a step further and invest some of our winnings in a horse so we could all get together from time to time and have a bit of fun at the track watching the horse run and hopefully if we bought the right type of animal line it up for a gamble or two. We knew a trainer quite well who was very shrewd when it came to purchasing bargain basement horses and had some very knowledgeable contacts in Ireland, one of whom knew a trainer that had been lining this particular horse up for a touch on its handicap debut but the owner now wanted to sell it as he was becoming impatient and running out of funds. This sounded the right opportunity for us boys to buy it and if the story stacked up hopefully get some or all of our money back pretty quickly. The horse had not shown much at all in its native Ireland and form figures of 000 didn't tell the real story. We bought the horse for a fair price at the level of money we had planned to spend. Of course there would be training fees and other bills we had to pay and they were factored into the price, but from what we had been told by connections we felt we had purchased a winner waiting to happen and after the horse had shown up pretty well at home for its new trainer with some much higher rated galloping companions, you could say that it's new owners were rather pleased to say the least with the purchase. Our plan now looked likely to come into fruition and we were all getting pretty excited at the prospect of taking a large chunk of money from those poor unsuspecting bookies.

The horse had been entered in what can only be described as an egg and spoon race run at Wolverhampton on a very cold mid- winters evening when anyone in their right mind would be sat at home with the central heating on full blast. The trainer had asked if we would like to book his yard apprentice for the ride, who to be fair had ridden a few winners and placed horses at the track and we would have the extra insurance of the jockeys seven pound claim which should greatly enhance the horses chance of winning and if the combination got along maybe would run up a sequence of wins. That's how well handicapped the trainer thought the horse was on the night running against some very low grade totally exposed opposition. The plan was set in motion and the money went on big time each way at odds as big as 25/1 and below. We had thoughts of covering our purchase price, training fees and the planned party afterwards all in one go, as defeat was considered out of the question.

The horse was well drawn on the inside but slowly away the inexperienced jockey kept the horse tight against the inside running rail waiting and hoping for gaps that never appeared for him to make a challenge. We didn't even get our place money as the horse finished a close up hard held sixth, If things had panned out as planned our long term plan would have been a very lucrative one. The run didn't go unnoticed by the form students and went down in many notebooks as an eye catching debut run. We did however manage to get some of our money back next time out when the horse was ridden by the course top jockey to win at considerably shorter odds given a beautiful ride and the result was never in doubt, the horse followed up under the same jockey just two days later. From that day on we have only ever backed what we consider to be **TOP JOCKEYS** and here is the process we go through to find our very lucrative selections.

CONTENTS

Modus Operandi	6
Course Top Jockeys Mounts	17
Jockey Bookings	18
Expert Advice / Form Study / Video Form	22
Spotlight	24
Final Selection Results	31
Summary of Method to Date	32
The Theory	34
Unexposed / Exposed Runners	40
Additional Notable Information	51
One Trick Jockey	55
One Trick Trainers	58
Market Movers	66
Betfair V Bookmakers	68
Backers Mindset	71
Banking and Staking	75
Disclaimer	76
Results	78

MODUS OPERANDI

When I first started betting on horses seriously from the age of around 19, there was not the volume of low grade racing there is today. During the week there was normally two to three meetings and on a Saturday maybe four and can you believe we all got a day off on Sundays as there was no racing!! To be honest I don't really get why there is so much racing now, and from a personal point of view I would like to see a lot less but better quality racing. This would suit us punters better than the bookmakers who love the fact there is plenty of this low grade dross which we have at the moment as the lower the grade the more likely there are to be shock results, as it is easier for connections to lay a horse out to win a bad race than a good one (if the plan comes off!!)

There is only so much money around and whether that is bet on two meetings or seven meetings, people cannot just pluck money out of thin air to bet with. This week in the news the government stated that they are looking to ban the use of credit cards to bet with and that is a fantastic move coming after they reduced the amounts allowed to be staked in the fixed odds betting terminals finally giving back some credibility to the betting industry as there are many lives ruined for people who simply cannot control their urge to have a bet.

As much as I love the sport I think it has been downgraded over the years by the number of meetings we have to cope with each day, the fact is that no one can bet in each and every race in a single day of the week unless you are on a self - destruct mission or simply have a bottomless betting bank. I don't fall into either category but would like to fall into the latter. There are of course ways of getting around this deluge of racing without getting drawn into the drudgery of endless boring form study and still operate a profitable more exciting approach and this goes back to what I mentioned earlier about only backing top jockeys or in our case top course jockeys, by joining in on their success and taking more selective approach to your selection process and betting.

If you consider on a busy Saturday especially in the summer months there may be seven meetings in the day with sometimes seven races at each course so if the average field size was ten runners you are looking at 490 runners on the day, even with computerised form and ratings etc. I have absolutely no appetite to have to go through so much racing. My approach now and has been for quite some time is to only look at the COURSE TOP JOCKEY on any given day at each meeting and analyse his or her mounts on that day. It is of course possible that a top jockey will be in high demand especially on a Saturday, but even so if they had a mount in every race on the day (which is highly unlikely) you have immediately cut the number of runners to look at from 490 to 49.

There are of course many different approaches to finding winners and believe me I have tried just about every angle there is, but can say I have found a method here that works for me which doesn't throw up too many selections each day, which can also be if you want it to be very, very selective, meaning you would only be backing the very strongest selections that will provide you with a range of good priced winners from a range of prices from very short priced favourites (which you may choose to overlook), to some extremely high priced winners which to be honest is beyond me how they win at such long odds given that they are ridden by the course top jockeys yet overlooked by the betting public. But when you go through this method some of the course top jockeys may very well surprise you and that's the reason their runners may well be overlooked and overpriced.

Now look at the scenario below from a typical midweek meeting on the 17th of January 2020.

Information taken from the Racing Post online digital and paper version which you will need to subscribe to or purchase the paper version daily to operate this method.

CHEPSTOW TOP JOCKEYS

Jumps 2015/16+

WINS-RIDES	TRAINER SUPPLYING RIDES TODAY GIVING BEST COURSE RECORD WINS-RIDES	ALL RIDES SINCE £1 STAKE	COURSE RIDES WIN
42-183 23% Richard Johnson [2]	Rebecca Curtis 1-5 20%	+31.13	6

1/2 PORT OF MARS (IRE) [20] — 4
b g Westerner-Sarahall
Olly Murphy [2] Noel And Valerie Moran
t[1] 6 11-4
[1]Richard Johnson (120)

3247/42 JUST A THOUGHT (IRE) [*2 s2] — 2
ch m Stowaway-Carrig Lucy
Rebecca Curtis Hyde, Outhart, Moran And Hill
p[1] 8 11-12
Richard Johnson (126)

The top jockey riding at Chepstow today is Richard Johnson who has a total of two mounts on the day

MUSSELBURGH TOP JOCKEYS

Jumps 2015/16 +

WINS-RIDES		TRAINER SUPPLYING RIDES TODAY GIVING BEST COURSE RECORD	WINS-RIDES		ALL RIDES £1 STAKE	COURSE RIDES SINCE WIN
50-215	23% Brian Hughes [5]	Keith Dalgleish	16-40	40%	−12.90	1

4   5-34452 **HIGHWAY COMPANION** (IRE) [16] BF   t6 11-7
b g Milan-Niffyrann   Brian Hughes
Keith Dalgleish   Waldspec Glasgow Limited   (121)

4   33 **ROYAL COSMIC** [20]   6 11-0
b m Wootton Bassett-Cosmic Case   Brian Hughes
Richard Fahey   The Cosmic Cases   (115)

3   112-32 **KAJAKI** (IRE) [34] D1   7 11-7
gr g Mastercraftsman-No Quest   Brian Hughes
Nicky Richards[2]   F Gillespie   (133)

7   5-5F62P **PC DIXON** [15] S1   7 10-12
ch g Sixties Icon-Lakaam   'Brian Hughes
Victor Thompson   V Thompson   (108)

1   2-11 **CHUVELO** (IRE) [35] S2   5 12-0
b g Milan-Bargante   Brian Hughes
Donald McCain   T G Leslie   (121)

The top jockey riding at Musselburgh today is Brian Hughes who has a total of five mounts on the day

TOP JOCKEY

NEWCASTLE (AW) TOP JOCKEYS
Flat 2016+

WINS-RIDES		TRAINER SUPPLYING RIDES TODAY GIVING BEST COURSE RECORD	WINS-RIDES		COURSE RIDES ALL RIDES £1 STAKE	RIDES SINCE WIN
65-398	16% Ben Curtis [8]	Roger Fell	7-38	18%	+19.55	0

563806- STRICT (IRE) [46]
4 b g Slade Power-Thawrah
(1) Michael Appleby Honestly Racing
p 4 9-6
[1]Ben Curtis (68)

477939- SIR GNET (IRE) [34]
1 b g Galileo-Ecoutta
(10) Ed Dunlop Quentin Zheng
6 9-8
Ben Curtis (68)

330577- KUPA RIVER (IRE) [34 D1 S1]
6 b g Big Bad Bob-Lamanka Lass
(8) Roger Fell Middleham Park Racing Lxxii & Partner
h 6 9-4
Ben Curtis (91)

45454-1 DOUBLE MARTINI (IRE) (5ex) [8 F1 CD1]
1 ch c Mastercraftsman-Dusty Moon
(10) Roger Fell Middleham Park, Ventura Racing&partners
4 9-11
Ben Curtis (78)

839270- VENTUROUS (IRE) [118 D1 F1]
2 ch g Raven's Pass-Bold Desire
(3) David Barron Laurence O'Kane/Harrowgate Bloodstock Ltd
7 9-0
Ben Curtis (109)

2- TOMMY DE VITO [10] [74]
4 b c Dandy Man-Rohindi
(1) Charles Hills Chelsea Thoroughbreds - Goodfellas
3 9-5
[1]Ben Curtis (76)

256140- BLACK FRIDAY [42 S1]
5 b g Equiano-The Clan Macdonald
(4) Karen McLintock Miss S A Booth & Don Eddy
p 5 9-6
[1]Ben Curtis (88)

888435- SHE'S EASYONTHEEYE (IRE) [84 BF]
5 b f Kodiac-Bonnie Lesley
(5) John Quinn The Odd One Out Partnership
3 8-9
[1]Ben Curtis (73)

The top jockey riding at Newcastle today is Ben Curtis who has a total of eight mounts on the day

TOP JOCKEY

The top jockey riding at Lingfield (AW) today is Luke Morris who has a total of six mounts on the day

Following all of the top jockeys mounts today blindly would mean that in total you would have had to back a total of twenty one runners. It is unusual that a jockey will have a booked ride in every race which Ben Curtis has managed to do and it is very unlikely that he would go through the card at Newcastle today but it does go to show how high in demand these top jockeys are and I have to say that I have been very impressed by this jockey, more than any other this winter and totally get why he is in such high demand and I can tell you he has made me plenty of money too by backing him at all of the all weather tracks this winter and can see him continuing to build on this now in the coming 2020 flat turf season.

TOP JOCKEY

So let's now take a look and see how we would have fared betting blindly on all of these top jockeys mounts today

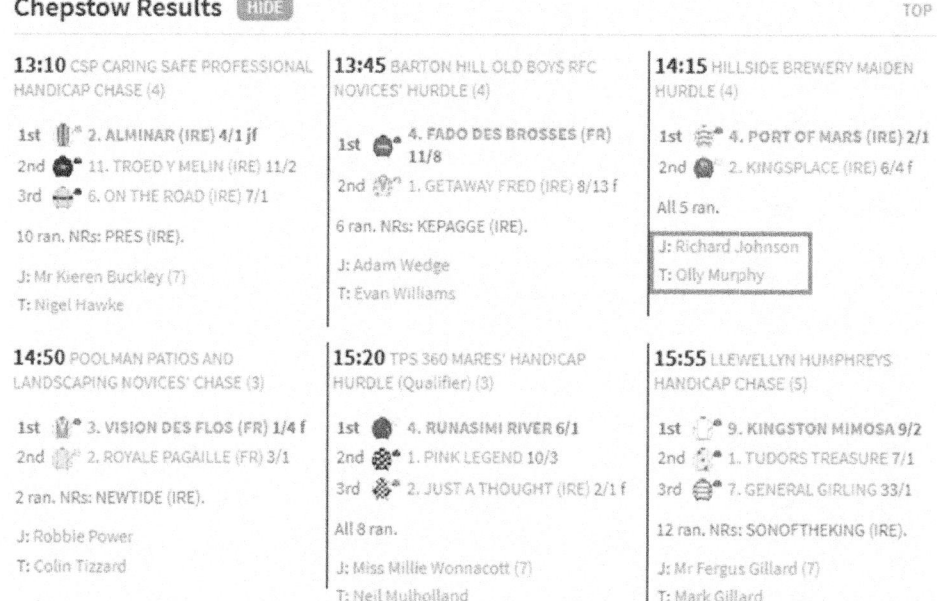

RICHARD JOHNSON ONE WINNER FROM HIS TWO MOUNTS +1 POINT LEVEL STAKES PROFIT ON THE DAY

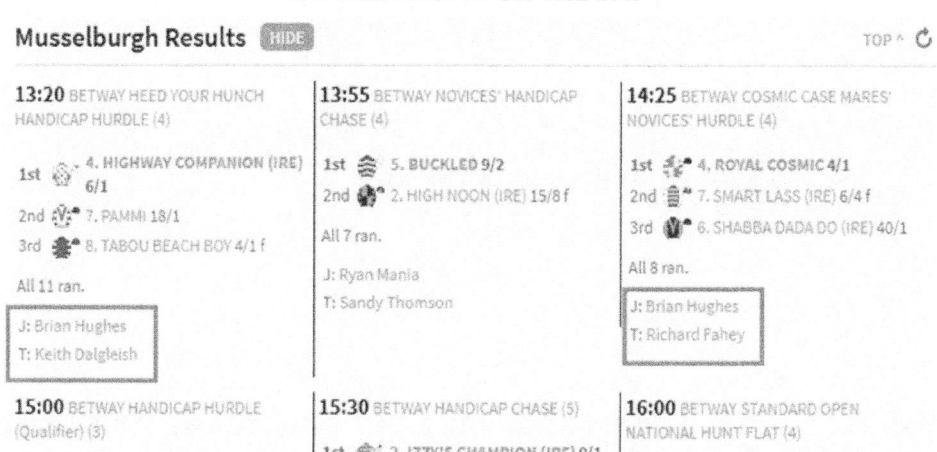

TOP JOCKEY

1st 7. THE MOUSE DOCTOR (IRE) 6/4 f	2nd 3. CARRIED (IRE) 9/2	1st 3. GOOD TIME JONNY (IRE) 5/6 f
2nd 5. SEABOROUGH (IRE) 11/2	3rd 8. STORMBAY BOMBER (IRE) 7/1	2nd 1. CHUVELO (IRE) 5/4
3rd 3. KAJAKI (IRE) 13/5	All 9 ran.	All 7 ran.
8 ran. NRs: MISTER MANDURO (FR).	J: Stephen Mulqueen (3)	J: Philip Enright
J: Philip Enright	T: Lucinda Russell	T: A. J. Martin, Ireland
T: A. J. Martin, Ireland		

BRIAN HUGHES TWO WINNERS FORM HIS 5 MOUNTS +7 POINTS LEVEL STAKES PROFIT ON THE DAY

Newcastle Results

15:15 BETWAY HEED YOUR HUNCH HANDICAP (6) (D.I)	**15:45** BETWAY HEED YOUR HUNCH HANDICAP (6) (D.II)	**16:15** BOMBARDIER BRITISH HOPPED AMBER BEER HANDICAP (4)
1st 1. FORESEE (GER) 8/15 f	1st 6. ACCESSOR (IRE) 11/4 f	1st 1. FIRST RESPONSE 7/2
2nd 8. ATEESCOMPONENT (IRE) 40/1	2nd 5. FRAME RATE 33/1	2nd 2. PAPARAZZI 16/1
3rd 6. NEARLY THERE 9/1	3rd 3. SWEET MARMALADE (IRE) 5/1	3rd 8. INSURPLUS (IRE) 9/1
All 11 ran.	All 11 ran.	All 8 ran.
J: Elisha Whittington (7)	J: Joe Fanning	J: James Sullivan
T: Tony Carroll	T: Michael Wigham	T: Linda Stubbs

16:45 BOMBARDIER GOLDEN BEER HANDICAP (6)	**17:15** HEED YOUR HUNCH AT BETWAY HANDICAP (3)	**17:45** LADBROKES WHERE THE NATION PLAYS NOVICE STAKES (4)
1st 6. CURFEWED (IRE) 17/2	1st 2. VENTUROUS (IRE) 4/1	1st 4. TOMMY DE VITO 3/1
2nd 9. PROCEEDING 8/1	2nd 3. HEATH CHARNOCK 6/4 f	2nd 2. NEVER DARK 4/5 f
3rd 2. KIND REVIEW 25/1	All 6 ran.	All 6 ran.
All 10 ran.	J: Ben Curtis	J: Ben Curtis
J: Tom Eaves	T: David Barron	T: Charles Hills
T: Tracy Waggott		

18:15 PLAY 4 TO SCORE AT BETWAY HANDICAP (5)	**18:45** LADBROKES HOME OF THE ODDS BOOST HANDICAP (6)
1st 1. WASNTEXPECTINGTHAT 1/1 f	1st 2. COAST OFALFUJAIRAH (IRE) 5/2
2nd 10. BE PROUD (IRE) 9/1	2nd 1. KAYAT 9/4 f
3rd 9. ETIKAAL 13/2	7 ran. NRs: LEZARDRIEUX.
9 ran. NRs: ROCK BOY GREY (IRE) BLACK FRIDAY.	J: Tom Eaves
J: Barry McHugh	T: Kevin Ryan
T: Richard Fahey	

BEN CURTIS TWO WINNERS FROM HIS EIGHT MOUNTS +1 POINTS LEVEL STAKES PROFIT ON THE DAY

12

TOP JOCKEY

LUKE MORRIS ONE WINNER FROM HIS SIX MOUNTS +1 POINT LEVEL STAKES PROFIT ON THE DAY

It is very pleasing to see that all of the highlighted top jockeys had winners at their chosen tracks today and were all in profit. I hope you can now see the strength of the method. If we followed blindly ALL of the top jockeys mounts at each course today, Richard Johnson at Chepstow a winner at 2/1 and a level stakes profit of one point. Brian Hughes two winners from his five mounts making a profit of seven points. Ben Curtis, two winners from his eight mounts making a profit of one point and Luke Morris one winner from his six mounts making a profit of one point. An overall profit on the day of ten points backing them to level stakes. I think that any punter would be highly delighted making these kinds of profit on any day of the week, but of course this profit came from backing twenty one horses and no one would really want to be backing so many selections in a day. It was our initial bad experience with our failed betting coup that prompted us to research the Course top Jockeys and immediately noted the fantastic results they were achieving that made us want to look further into creating a method that did not overburden us with selections, yet still produced a good profit and from very little form study.

So we set ourselves a task each morning to scrutinise each and every runner that the course top jockeys are booked to ride and try to eliminate any horse that we consider to be out of form or totally exposed so basically simply making up the jockeys rides at the track on the day. It doesn't matter how good the jockey is, if a horse is fully exposed or out of form he or she will have to work wonders to get it to win, therefore it is likely to be beaten so scratched from our list of possible winners.

From watching various interviews on racing TV we know that most TOP jockeys possibly go to a track for one or maybe two mounts that have strong chances of winning and his or her agent will make up the mounts to as many as they possibly can by ringing trainers they have a good association with to get their jockey as many mounts on the day with a good chance of winning, note this final point WITH A GOOD CHANCE OF WINNING. The course a jockey would not want to be riding seven mounts on an afternoon followed by seven mounts at an evening meeting after riding out early doors for their retained yard as a jockey would soon burn themselves out following such a demanding schedule, therefore top jockeys try to be quite selective and this can work in our favour too.

If a trainer knows that Richard Johnson is riding at Chepstow and they have a runner with a big chance of winning they would love to get him on board to give their mount a better chance of winning. It is also great for the owners that they have a top class jockey riding their horse and for the photo shoot afterwards.

There are of course trainers the top jockeys use more than others and these trainers are the ones likely to give them a winner on the day and more likely than not the reason the jockey has gone to that particular course on this particular day. It is these top jockey / trainer combinations that we look at and eliminate their other mounts, therefore making the method more selective.

Many top jockeys have retainers from top trainers and they must ride for this yard whether the horse has a chance or not. Again we must go through the form of these runners as a top jockey / top stable does not guarantee success but it's a combination to have on your side. It is impossible to equate how much a top jockey is worth at a course, but these jockeys know the track inside out and at a course such as Ling field with its tight final bend, you often see jockeys such as Adam Kirby or Luke Morris gain a length or two by being in the right position to swing off this final bend and make their run to the line only to hold on by a whisker, priceless from a punters point of view as it must also be for the owners and trainers.

Now let's go through the above list of jockeys and trainers again to basically show you the horses that we would have eliminated on the day and the ones we would have backed and the reasons why. The first information we look at are the COURSE JOCKEY TABLES IN THE RACING POST PAPER VERSION

CHEPSTOW TOP JOCKEYS

Jumps 2015/16+

WINS-RIDES	TRAINER SUPPLYING RIDES TODAY GIVING BEST COURSE RECORD	WINS-RIDES	%	ALL RIDES £1 STAKE	COURSE RIDES SINCE WIN
42-183	23% Richard Johnson ² .... Rebecca Curtis	1-5	20%	+31.13	6
21-115	18% Sam Twiston-Davies ¹ ....Nigel Twiston-Davies	5-28	18%	-38.00	11
19-114	17% Tom Scudamore ³ ....David Pipe	8-41	20%	-3.30	5
18-133	14% Adam Wedge ³ ....Evan Williams	15-100	15%	+21.41	2
12-83	14% Tom O'Brien ² ....Robert Stephens	0-7	0%	-10.81	6

As you can see from the Top Jockeys table at Chepstow that **Richard Johnson** is the top jockey riding today he has two mounts (2) after his name, the trainer supplying him with the most wins to rides at the track today is **Rebecca Curtis** – We must make a note of any horses he rides for this trainer

MUSSELBURGH TOP JOCKEYS
Jumps 2015/16+

WINS-RIDES	%	Jockey	Trainer Supplying Rides Today Giving Best Course Record	WINS-RIDES	%	ALL RIDES £1 STAKE	COURSE RIDES SINCE WIN
50-215	23%	Brian Hughes 5	Keith Dalgleish	16-40	40%	−12.90	1
9-99	9%	Henry Brooke 3	Rebecca Menzies	1-1	100%	−26.67	2
8-93	9%	Craig Nichol 3	Keith Dalgleish	2-17	12%	−53.54	16
7-31	23%	Ryan Day 1	Iain Jardine	1-3	33%	+26.13	0
7-96	7%	Callum Bewley 2	Jim Goldie	4-33	12%	−24.50	3
5-38	13%	Dale Irving 2	Karen McLintock	1-3	33%	+28.00	5

The top jockey at Musselburgh is **Brian Hughes** (5) who has five mounts and the trainer supplying him with most wins – rides today is **Keith Dalgleish** again we must make a note of this combinations runners

NEWCASTLE (AW) TOP JOCKEYS
Flat 2016+

WINS-RIDES	%	Jockey	Trainer Supplying Rides Today Giving Best Course Record	WINS-RIDES	%	ALL RIDES £1 STAKE	COURSE RIDES SINCE WIN
65-398	16%	Ben Curtis 8	Roger Fell	7-38	18%	+19.55	0
54-394	14%	Joe Fanning 3	Mark Johnston	14-130	11%	−61.28	15
45-471	10%	Andrew Mullen 3	Ben Haslam	16-79	20%	−47.33	4
39-222	18%	Callum Rodriguez 3	Michael Dods	12-51	24%	+73.31	7
30-410	7%	Paul Mulrennan 6	Ben Haslam	6-42	14%	−181.95	3
29-460	6%	Graham Lee 1	Andrew Balding	0-7	0%	−239.69	1
25-312	8%	Phil Dennis 6	Rebecca Bastiman	1-5	20%	+20.23	10

The top jockey at Newcastle (AW) is **Ben Curtis** (8) who has eight mounts and the trainer supplying him with most wins – rides today is **Roger Fell** again make a note of this combination and their runners

LINGFIELD (AW) TOP JOCKEYS
Flat 2016+

WINS-RIDES	%	Jockey	Trainer Supplying Rides Today Giving Best Course Record	WINS-RIDES	%	ALL RIDES £1 STAKE	COURSE RIDES SINCE WIN
87-710	12%	Luke Morris 6	Sir Mark Prescott Bt	15-79	19%	−194.89	10
85-529	16%	Adam Kirby 4	David O'Meara	6-30	20%	−187.85	19
36-244	15%	Hollie Doyle 4	Archie Watson	12-45	27%	−0.84	1
36-264	14%	Robert Havlin 5	Michael Attwater	3-30	10%	−70.41	8
36-345	10%	David Probert 4	Simon Pearce	1-2	50%	−110.73	1
32-348	9%	Shane Kelly 3	George Baker	0-2	0%	−159.02	6

The top jockey at Ling field (AW) is **Luke Morris** (6) who has six mounts and the trainer supplying him with most wins - mounts today is **Sir Mark Prescott** we again make a note of this combination and their runners

COURSE TOP JOCKEYS MOUNTS

THE NEXT STEP TO FURTHER ELIMINATE JOCKEYS MOUNTS IS AS FOLLOWS

Go to the TRAINERSPOT section of the Racing Post (paper version only)

GB racing only on page 18 in the index below

Today

Interview: Jack Kennedy 6	Sales: Keeneland Wed Top 50 ... 79	Trainerspot .... GB 18; IRE 17
Horse Play 7	**ENTRIES & RESULTS**	Classifieds 19
Birthdays 9	Tomorrow 61	Naps Competition & Press
Markets 10	Sunday (declare today) 63	Challenge 73
Melrose On Betting 11	Tuesday 63	Statistics: Jumps 78
Top Tips 12	Early-closing races 64	Industry Information 79
Race of the day 12	Results 74	Overseas winners 79
Justin O'Hanlon 12		Going corrections 79
The Daily Briefing 12-13	**MISCELLANEOUS**	
Paul Kealy 13	Index to today's runners 10	Greyhounds 65
Favourites to focus on 13	Signposts .... GB 16; IRE 18	Racing Post Sport ..... back page
Yesterday at the races 14	Today's Trainers 16	Sport on TV 82
Point-to-Point Focus 14	Today's Jockeys 17	
Bloodstock World 15	Today's Flat Sires 18	

NOTE HERE THAT WE ARE ONLY INTERESTED IN GB RACING (exclude any Irish racing as we have enough on our plate following the meetings run in GB racing only)

JOCKEY BOOKINGS

The sections of further interest to us we are listed in the **jockey bookings** table

Jockey bookings

Significant jockey/trainer combinations, in profit to £1 bet;
BOLD *data — current season only; LIGHT — last four seasons, plus current.*
ⓒ *—data is course specific*
(therefore **bold** *data with* ⓒ *— today's course, current season).*
Flat season is defined as from January 1.
Includes those with more than one win, a strike-rate of at least 25% and a level-stakes profit.

LINGFIELD (AW)

6-15	40%	+£3.49	Adam Kirby/William Haggas	Quabil 12.00
2-6	33%	+£5.50	Grace McEntee/Stuart Williams	Haddaf 12.00
10-33	30%	+£35.92	ⓒAlistair Rawlinson/Michael Appleby	Barrington 12.00
4-12	33%	+£36.38	Hayley Turner/Charlie Fellowes	Golden Force 12.00
2-7	29%	+£10.00	ⓒJoey Haynes/Chelsea Banham	Axel Jacklin 12.30
2-7	29%	+£22.75	ⓒClifford Lee/David Evans	Brockey Rise 12.30; Mr Kodi 1.00
4-11	36%	+£10.76	Poppy Bridgwater/David Simcock	Inevitable Outcome 1.00
2-5	40%	+£1.13	ⓒHollie Doyle/Archie Watson	Quiet Word 1.35; Rhubarb Bikini 3.40
3-9	33%	+£10.25	Alistair Rawlinson/Robert Cowell	Savalas 2.05
2-4	50%	+£7.00	Darragh Keenan/John Ryan	Normal Norman 3.10
13-48	27%	+£6.63	ⓒJamie Spencer/David Simcock	Gregory K 3.40

NEWCASTLE (AW)

4-13	31%	+£2.50	ⓒJamie Gormley/Karen McLintock	
				Good Man 3.15; High Fort 4.45; Big Les 5.15
			2016+ 10-32 31% +£24.75	
2-4	50%	+£2.75	Elisha Whittington/Tony Carroll	Foresee 3.15
2-6	33%	+£25.00	Joe Fanning/Michael Wigham	Accessor 3.45
2-5	40%	+£4.50	ⓒAndrew Mullen/Ben Haslam	Blazing Dreams 4.45; Epeius 6.15
3-6	50%	+£13.37	ⓒBen Curtis/Charles Hills	Tommy De Vito 5.45
			2016+ 6-17 35% +£12.25	
6-24	25%	+£14.48	Graham Lee/Andrew Balding	Never Dark 5.45
2-8	25%	+£3.50	Ben Curtis/Karen McLintock	Black Friday 6.15
7-27	26%	+£11.25	ⓒBarry McHugh/Richard Fahey	Wasnexpectingthat 6.15
2-8	25%	+£6.00	Ben Curtis/John Quinn	She's Easyontheeye 6.45

CHEPSTOW

2-7	29%	+£32.00	Bryan Carver/Ron Hodges	Daytime Ahead 3.20

MUSSELBURGH

3-6	50%	+£13.75	Henry Brooke/Rebecca Menzies	Tabou Beach Boy 1.20
16-40	40%	+£17.17	ⓒBrian Hughes/Keith Dalgleish	Highway Companion 1.20
4-12	33%	+£43.75	Craig Nichol/Alistair Whillans	Abouttimeyoutoldme 1.20
2-6	33%	+£2.33	ⓒSam Coltherd/Stuart Coltherd	Warendorf 1.55; Graystown 3.30
5-15	33%	+£72.63	Sam Coltherd/William Young Jnr	Ardera Cross 3.00
4-12	33%	+£8.09	Dale Irving/Karen McLintock	Weather Front 3.00
2-6	33%	+£15.00	ⓒNathan Moscrop/Rebecca Menzies	Stormbay Bomber 3.30

TOP JOCKEY

We again make notes of our top jockeys at each meeting and who they are riding for in this JOCKEY BOOKINGS section, note that they may be the same trainers that are mentioned on the Course Jockey table but they also may be different additional trainers

We have noted that Richard Johnson riding at Chepstow has two mounts today and the trainer from the course jockey list is **Rebecca Curtis.** There are no further trainers to note from the Jockey bookings table so therefore if the form of the Rebecca Curtis horse stacks up that will be the only horse of Johnsons we back today

RICHARD JOHNSONS ONLY MOUNT TODAY

3247/42 **JUST A THOUGHT** (IRE) ⁷² ˢ²   p¹ 8 11-12
2   ch m Stowaway-Carrig Lucy   Richard Johnson
Rebecca Curtis   Hyde, Outhart, Moran And Hill   (126)

We have noted that Brian Hughes riding at Musselburgh has five mounts today and the trainer from the course jockey list is **Keith Dalgleish**, there are no further trainers to note from the Jockey bookings table and Hughes has just the one mount for the above mentioned trainer so therefore if the form of the Keith Dalgleish horse stacks up that will be the only horse of Hughes we back today.

BRIAN HUGHES ONLY MOUNT TODAY

5-34452 **HIGHWAY COMPANION** (IRE) ¹⁶ ᴮᶠ   t 6 11-7
4   b g Milan-Niffyrann   Brian Hughes
Keith Dalgleish   Weldspec Glasgow Limited   (121)

We have noted that Ben Curtis riding at Newcastle (AW) has a full book of eight rides today and the trainer from the course jockey list is **Roger Fell (two mounts)** but there are further trainers to note from the Jockey bookings table **Charlie Hills, Karen Mclintock and John Quinn** therefore if the form of all **five horse runners** stacks up then we may be backing this jockey these on these other runners today.

BEN CURTIS MOUNTS TODAY

330577- **KUPA RIVER** (IRE) 34 D1 S1 — h6 9-4
6 (8) — *b g Big Bad Bob-Lamanka Lass* — Ben Curtis (91)
Roger Fell Middleham Park Racing Lxxii & Partner

45454-1 **DOUBLE MARTINI** (IRE) (5ex) 8 F1 CD1 — 4 9-11
1 (10) — *ch c Mastercraftsman-Dusty Moon* — Ben Curtis (78)
Roger Fell Middleham Park, Ventura Racing&partners

256140- **BLACK FRIDAY** 42 S1 — p5 9-6
5 (4) — *b g Equiano-The Clan Macdonald* — 1Ben Curtis (88)
Karen McLintock Miss S A Booth & Don Eddy

2- **TOMMY DE VITO** 74 — 3 9-5
4 (1) — *b c Dandy Man-Rohlindi* — 1Ben Curtis (76)
Charles Hills Chelsea Thoroughbreds - Goodfellas

888435- **SHE'S EASYONTHEEYE** (IRE) 84 BF — 3 8-9
5 (5) — *b f Kodiac-Bonnie Lesley* — 1Ben Curtis (73)
John Quinn The Odd One Out Partnership

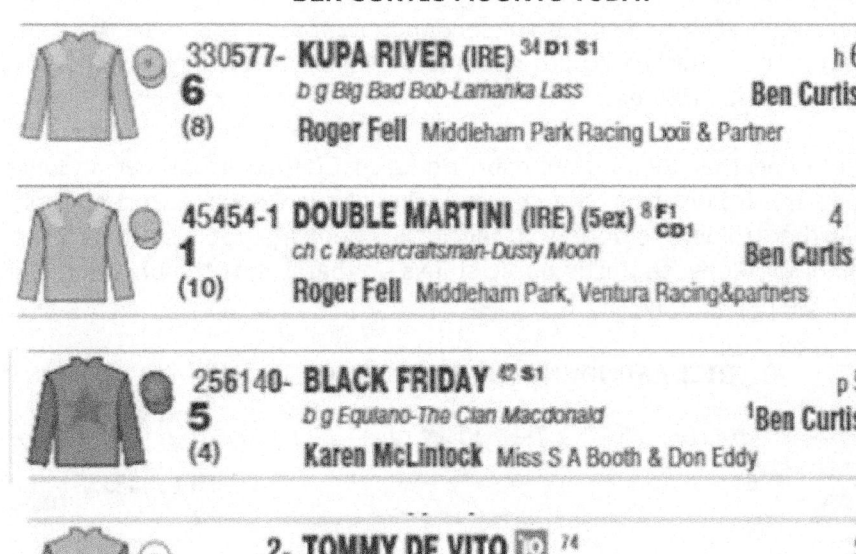

We have noted that Luke Morris riding at Ling field (AW) has six mounts today and the trainer from the course jockey list is **Mark Prescott,** there are no further trainers to note from the Jockey bookings table so therefore if the form of the Mark Prescott horse stacks up that will be the only horse of Morris we back today.

LUKE MORRIS ONLY MOUNT TODAY

679-2 **CLIFF WIND** 9 — p1 3 9-9
1 (9) — *gr f Invincible Spirit-Fork Lightning* — Luke Morris (64)
Sir Mark Prescott Bt Denford Stud

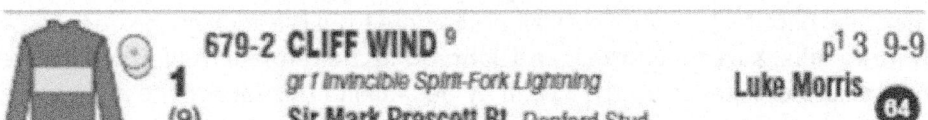

You can now see that immediately we have cut down the possible selections on the day down from twenty one to a possible eight, some of these runners too may be eliminated when we go on to examine the form.

We now need to look at our final list of possible selections to see if they have a good chance of winning their races today, and to possibly cut the list down even further by taking a delve into the possible selections form and their chance of winning today's race and to do so we add these further steps and the points listed in the below section.

EXPERT ADVICE / FORM STUDY / VIDEO FORM

1- NEVER BE AFRAID TO TAKE A LITTLE ADVICE FROM THE FORM EXPERTS
2- STUDY THE FORM YOURSELF
3- BELIEVE IN WHAT YOU KNOW AND YOU SEE

I have been seriously involved in racing in one guise or another for more than 40 years, as a part time pundit, syndicate manager, website owner and professional backer, the last ten years or so more of the latter, yet it doesn't matter how much you know about form and what looks good form or not so good. It is always good to seek a second opinion. I don't have friends who work in the same sphere as myself who I can call up and ask for advice about a particular runner on any given day and don't get me wrong I would not do this anyway as I consider myself to be a very good judge and value my own opinion far greater than anyone else's, but sometimes I may doubt myself or go through phases (especially if I hit a losing run) and a good trusted second opinion helps. publications such as the Racing Post or Timeform which we are already using to get our initial selections from, so why not put the publication to further use? They generally have a couple of form experts who go through a card each day and go through the form with a fine tooth comb so their opinion is well worth a read. This is their SPOTLIGHT section of the paper where each runner has been analysed and an opinion based on form is given on its chances in the race.

NEVER FOLLOW TIPSTERS from the paper this paper or any other in fact as tipsters have to make a selection in every race on each day which takes us back to our busy Saturday. How can a tipster select 49 credible selections in a day!!

Another site I greatly respect is www.timeform.comTheir analysis of the form as you would expect is also very good and another good reference point before making up your mind as whether to place a bet or not. A word of caution here, we are only looking at their analysis of our runners chance not what they think will win the race or not. When they give a selection for the race they may overlook the horse that has the best form if it's a short price and give what they consider to be a value alternative. We are looking for horses with good solid form so remember that it is their summary of our horses chance rather than their selection we are interested in. it's all well and good looking for value bets, there will be plenty of winners come our way at good prices out of this method. The shorter priced ones will keep our bank ticking along so don't get too engrossed with value.

The best section of racing post online is their video form which can be accessed in their form pages. To me this has more value than the written form or any experts opinion so again if you are subscribing to the racing post then make use of this facility. It's amazing how many times I read an experts view on a horses past performance then watch are run only to find myself totally disagreeing with the experts take on the race. It doesn't happen often but the fact it does means it is a process you must go through and this is a thoroughly rewarding exercise that can really throw up some fantastic winners. For instance, you may think the horse didn't get the clearest of runs but the expert has overlooked this, you may see a horse running on late or given a poor or considerate ride, this may not be mentioned in the form pages of the post or by the experts. If you can learn to read past races it is better than browsing through any form book believe me.

Our final process will be based on the actual written form and ratings to see if the horse looks exposed or unexposed and the only way of doing so is to study the horses past form and ratings. Unexposed horses are the ones who are likely to supply our jockeys with most of their winners. Thoroughly exposed horses are unlikely to win regardless of the jockeys talent in the saddle.

SPOTLIGHT

SPOTLIGHT

COMMENTS FROM THE RACING POST

Just A Thought Missed last season but built upon encouraging reappearance run when second here (2m7f, soft) in November; handed a 5lb rise but today's drop back in trip won't be a problem; big player if first-time cheekpieces have any sort of positive effect.

Just A Thought 11-12

8-y-o ch m Stowaway - Carrig Lucy (Phardante)
Rebecca Curtis   Richard Johnson

Placings: 2/113/2223247/42

	Starts	1st	2nd	3rd	Win & Pl
OR **125**					
Hurdles	9	–	5	1	£9,840
All Jumps races	12	2	5	2	£15,489
12/16 Hrfd	2m Cls6 NHF 3-6yo soft (M)				£1,560
11/16 Ffos	2m Cls6 NHF 4-6yo soft (M)				£1,949
				Total win prize-money	£3,509

Good 0-0-1 Gd-Sft 0-2-2 Soft 2-6-9 Class 3 0-1-1
Course 0-2-3 Dist 0-1-3 LeftH 1-6-9 RightH 1-2-3
TmOfYr 0-1-1 Jockey 1-1-2

Having had a thorough look at this horse's lifeTimeform on the Racing Post website and watched past recordings of its races it's doesn't look like a winner waiting to happen and as an eight year old with form figures of 3/2223247/42 since its last win the number of seconds looks to me like the horse does not know how to win, I have left this one out of my calculations today even though it has a fairly positive comment by the Racing Posts Spotlight.

SP☼TLIGHT

COMMENTS FROM THE RACING POST

Highway Companion Still looking for first win over hurdles but produced his best effort so far when chasing home Not The Chablis over C&D (good to soft) 16 days ago; 2lb better off for a beating of less than a length so nothing to choose between the pair.

Highway Companion 11-7

6-y-o b g Milan - Niffyrann (Sheyrann)
Keith Dalgleish — Brian Hughes

Placings: P2/25-34452

OR 109

	Starts	1st	2nd	3rd	Win & Pl
Hurdles	5	-	1	1	£3,431
All Jumps races	7	-	2	1	£4,385

Gd-Sft 0-1-3 Soft 0-2-3 Heavy 0-0-1 Class 4 0-3-6
Course 0-1-1 Dist 0-1-1 LeftH 0-2-6 RightH 0-1-1
T-strp 0-1-2 Jockey 0-2-3

1 Jan Musselburgh 2nd, see NOT THE CHABLIS

8 Dec 19 Kelso 2m Cls4 94-109 Hdl Hcap £4,289
14 ran SOFT   8hdls   Time 4m 17.61s (s/w 34.61s)
1 Temple Man 7 11-6 ....Jamie Hamilton 7/1
2 Rubytwo 7 11-0 ......Danny McMenamin (5) 9/4F
3 Bloorledotcom 4 11-0 h ..Blair Campbell (3) 28/1
5 HIGHWAY COMPANION 5 11-11 ht¹ ....
..............................Brian Hughes 3/1
chased leader, lost second but close up 3rd, ridden 3 out, outpaced from 2 out
btn 8½ lgths [RPR105 TS84 OR108] [op 7/2]

Dist: 3-3-½-2-2¾   RACE RPR: 111+/105/99
NEXT RUN: First 3 w1 p0 u1 Also rans w1 p1 u5

9 Nov 19 Kelso 2m5f Cls4 103-122 Hdl Hcap £4,938
9 ran HEAVY   11hdls   Time 5m 47.50s (s/w 57.50s)
1 Spirit Of Kayf 8 11-8 t¹ ....Bruce Lynn (7) 4/1
2 Bally Conor 6 11-12 ....Henry Brooke 5/1
3 Put The Law On You 4 10-10 p Callum Bowley 20/1
4 HIGHWAY COMPANION 5 11-2 h ....
..............................Sean Quinlan 11/4F
held up, steady headway before 2 out, ridden between last 2, soon no impression
btn 7¼ lgths [RPR109 TS43 OR109][op 5/2 tchd 9/4]

Dist: 1¾-5-½-1¼-15   RACE RPR: 128+/123+/103
NEXT RUN: First 3 w1 p0 u1 Also rans w0 p1 u4

1 Jan Musselburgh 2m4f Cls4 89-107 Hdl Hcap £5,588
12 ran GD-SFT   12hdls   Time 5m 6.60s (s/w 31.60s)
1 NOT THE CHABLIS 6 10-11 p Lucy Alexander 11/2
made virtually all, ridden and hard pressed from 3 out, bumped before last, kept on well run-in, gamely [RPR95 TS27 OR92]   [tchd 5/1]
2 HIGHWAY COMPANION 6 11-12 t ....
..............................Brian Hughes 3/1F
took keen hold, close up, challenging going easily 3 out, ridden and hung left from 2 out, kept on run-in
btn ¾ lgths [RPR110 TS41 OR107][op 7/2 tchd 100/30 & 4/1]
3 Chosen Flame 8 10-9 ....Craig Nichol 7/1
4 LASTOFTHECOSMICS 5 10-12 t ....
..............................Callum Bowley 12/1

It is this horses last race that looks the key to its chance today and the comment **produced its best effort so far** make this runner of interest, it was beaten by Not the Chablis last time out but was keen early on and looked the likely winner on the replay of this race, its better off with the winner so I will be making this one a bet today.

TOP JOCKEY

SP✸TLIGHT

COMMENTS FROM THE RACING POST

Kupa River Triple turf winner at up to 1m; has run with credit here, and was a 6f Tapeta winner at Wolverhampton last March; ended last year with two below-par runs (6f/7f) but current mark is workable.

This horse had won previously from its current mark which is always a positive and was possibly a little unlucky watching the race again as it was slowly away, pulled too hard and denied a clear run so would certainly give it a chance to make amends here.

COMMENTS FROM THE RACING POST

Double Martini Ex-Irish colt who has edged down the weights since joining Roger Fell and took advantage in C&D handicap last week, proving suited by the step up to 1m; not obviously well-in under his 5lb penalty but it wouldn't be any surprise if he's got more to offer over this trip; should go close at the least.

This horse although given a positive by Spotlight, could follow up but I was not that impressed by its win last time out on the replay of the race and has to run from a 5lb higher mark here which I think makes it vulnerable so will not be backing it today.

SPOTLIGHT

COMMENTS FROM THE RACING POST

Black Friday Landed 7f Musselburgh handicap in October but he's winless from five goes on the AW and came home last of 14 over C&D last month; he has something to prove now.

A negative comment form Spotlight so I won't pursue this as a selection

SPOTLIGHT

COMMENTS FROM THE RACING POST

Tommy de Vito Showed clear ability when second on C&D debut 74 days ago; that bare form isn't anything to write home about but he's open to progress.

Tommy de Vito	9-5

3-y-o b c Dandy Man (6.4f) - Rohlindi (Red Ransom) £35,000 Y; fourth foal; half-brother to 8.4f/1m2f winner War Of Succession (RPR 89) and 5f winner Mistress Of Venice (99); dam placed 5.7f (68), half-sister to 7f Listed winner Kalindi (dam of Medicean Man) out of 5f/6f 2yo winner

Charles Hills   Ben Curtis

Placings: 2-				Draw: 1
	Starts	1st	2nd 3rd	Win & Pl
All Flat races	1	-	1 -	£827

Stand 0-1-1 Course 0-1-1 Dist 0-1-1

4 Nov 19 Newcastle (AW) 6f Cls6 Auct 2yo £2,782
9 ran   STAND   Time 1m 14.79s (slw 4.39s)
1 Asmund 2 9-5 p¹ ....Ben Curtis ¹ 4/11F
2 **TOMMY DE VITO** 2 9-5 ......P J McDonald ⁷ 4/1
   dwelt, held up behind leading group, headway to press winner over 1f out, ridden and one pace inside final furlong
    btn 1¼ lgths [RPR67 TS10]   [tchd 9/2]
3 Grandads Best Girl 2 9-0 ...Ben Robinson ³ 40/1
Dist: 1¼-1¼-1¾-1¾-¾   RACE RPR: 71+/67/58
NEXT RUN: **First** 3 w0 p1 u0 Also rans w0 p0 u2

Probably the most unexposed runner of the day this system has thrown up, comment **open to progress** this is the type of horse I love to bet if I can make a strong case for them and although only second on debut it was against a long odds on shot ridden by today's jockey which is an interesting angle alone, must be given a chance to improve so I will be backing this.

SPTLIGHT

COMMENTS FROM THE RACING POST

She's Easyontheeye Proven over C&D but she remains winless after nine outings and needs to return fully tuned up after 84-day break if she's to contend for a first success.

A negative comment from spotlight, winless after nine starts and returning from a break not the profile of a horse I want to back.

SP TLIGHT

COMMENTS FROM THE RACING POST

Cliff Wind No better than midfield in three quick qualifying runs but she showed more when second of ten at Kempton on last week's handicap debut; held every chance there but her inexperience was evident under pressure; more to come and the headgear might help her focus where it matters.

Cliff Wind	9-9
3-y-o gr f Invincible Spirit (7.4f) - Fork Lightning (Storm Cat)	
Sir Mark Prescott Bt	Luke Morris
Placings: 679-2	Draw: 9

OR56	Starts	1st	2nd	3rd	Win & Pl
All Flat races	4	–	1	–	£924

Stand 0-0-3 Std-Slw 0-1-1 Class 6 0-1-1 Dist 0-1-2
LeftH 0-0-2 RightH 0-1-1 TmOfYr 0-1-1 Jockey 0-1-4

8 Jan Kempton (AW) 6f Cls6 45-67 3yo Hcap £3,105
10 ran STD-SLW Time 1m 14.09s (slw 3.59s)
1 Miss Thoughtful 3 9-10 ....Nicola Currie 6 6/1
2 CLIFF WIND 3 8-13 ....Luke Morris 1 11/1
in touch in midfield, effort and headway 2f out, ridden to lead entering final furlong, hung left and headed well inside final furlong, kept on same pace towards finish (jockey said filly hung left-handed under pressure)
btn ¾ lgths [RPR59 TS41 OR56] [op 12/1 tchd 10/1]
3 STAR OF ST LOUIS 3 8-2 ...Kieran O'Neill 2 7/1
chased leaders, switched left and effort just over 2f out, switched back right 2f out, chased leading pair 1f out, no extra and outpaced well inside final furlong
btn 2½ lgths [RPR43 TS23 OR45] [tchd 6/1]

TOP JOCKEY

Dist: ¾-1¾-¾-1-1½   RACE RPR: 73/59/43
NEXT RUN: First 3 w0 p0 u0 Also rans w0 p0 u0

27 Dec 19 Wolverhampton (AW) 6f Cls5 2yo (F)
£3,429
12 ran STAND   Time 1m 14.75s (sts 2.95s)
1 Tomorrow's Dream 2 9-0 Tom Marquand [9] 100/30
2 Mountain Brave 2 9-0 ....Jack Mitchell [4] 33/1
3 Yukon Mission 2 9-0 ....Jason Hart [6] 11/1
9 CLIFF WIND 2 9-0 ....Luke Morris [1] 66/1
slowly into stride, held up, pulled hard, raced wide from halfway, shaken up over 1f out, never on terms btn 9 lgths [RPR48 TS3]   [op 80/1]
Dist: 1½-½-½-1-nse   RACE RPR: 75+/70/69
NEXT RUN: First 3 w0 p0 u3 Also rans w1 p1 u2

9 Dec 19 Newcastle (AW) 5f Cls5 2yo £3,429
9 ran STAND   Time 1m 0.17s (sts 2.17s)
1 Minhaaj 2 8-12 ....Ben Curtis [3] 8/13F
2 Gowanlad 2 9-3 ....Phil Dennis [1] 12/1
3 Lapses Linguae 2 8-12 ....Jason Hart [9] 3/1
7 CLIFF WIND 2 8-12 ....Luke Morris [7] 33/1
went right start, chased leaders, ridden along over 2f out, soon weakened
btn 6¾ lgths [RPR52 TS20]   [tchd 28/1]
Dist: 1½-2¼-nk-hd-¾   RACE RPR: 74+/75/61
NEXT RUN: First 3 w0 p0 u1 Also rans w0 p1 u2

18 Nov 19 Wolverhampton (AW) 5f Cls5 2yo £3,429
11 ran STAND   Time 59.76s (sts 0.16s)
1 Auchterarder 2 9-5 ....Jason Hart [4] 5/2
2 Rocking Reg 2 9-3 ....Jason Watson [10] 10/1
3 Minhaaj 2 8-12 ....Jim Crowley [3] 4/6F
6 CLIFF WIND 2 8-12 ....Luke Morris [9] 40/1
chased leaders, raced awkwardly, cajoled along 3f out, made no impression
btn 11 lgths [RPR37 TS26]   [op 33/1]
9 KNOCKACURRA 2 9-3 t1 ...Shane Kelly [2] 100/1
tracked leader, ridden and weakened from 2f out btn 12 lgths [RPR38 TS26]
Dist: 4-1-5-½-½   RACE RPR: 84/68/59+
NEXT RUN: First 3 w1 p2 u0 Also rans w0 p0 u7

This horse looked to be a Mark Prescott special, primed to strike first run in a handicap after some quiet runs, the money went astray last time out but a recovery mission looks on the cards so I will be backing this

FINAL SELECTION RESULTS

LIST OF FINAL SELECTIONS ON THE DAY

Going through the form and the Videos of past racing along with the comments from Spotlight I have decided to have four bets today

- 1 -   HIGHWAY COMPANION - *WON 6/1*
- 2 -   KUPA RIVER - *LOST*
- 3 -   TOMMY DE VITO - *WON 3/1*
- 4 -   CLIFF WIND – *LOST*

A FANTASTIC 7 POINTS PROFIT BETTING TO LEVEL STAKES BETTING ON FOUR VERY STRONG FORM SELECTIONS ALL RIDDEN BY THE COURSE TOP JOCKEYS

SUMMARY OF METHOD TO DATE

Our selections are derived each day using the following tried and trusted steps

1 - Go to each meeting each day and note the top jockey at the course and the trainer who is supplying him or her with the most wins to runners at the course. Note down the trainer and how many mounts the jockey has at the meeting riding for the named trainer.

2 - Go to the Trainer spot section in Racing Post and the Jockey bookings section and again note any trainer who has booked the top course jockey at the meeting, again note the horses name and time of the race.

3 - **Any other mounts the top jockey may have on the day can be ignored if not flagged up in the two sections mentioned above,** although the jockeys will have winners riding for trainers not mentioned in the above two sections we have to forfeit these in an effort to make the method more selective and concentrate on the jockey/trainer combinations that are proven to make a level stakes profit when they team up, the statistics on amount they have made to date and the strike rate are listed in the Jockey bookings table and the course top jockey tables.

4 - Check the SPOTLIGHT verdict of the possible selections chances in the Racing Post, this is found under the listed runners and riders for the race in the race card section, note any positive / negative comments. A strong positive about the horses chance is what we are looking for to make the horse a possible bet, a strong negative may make me put a line through the selection. If you require a second opinion on the horses chances or have any doubts go to www.timeform.com and to their race cards for this second opinion on the horses chance, a horse I am looking to back today has a positive chance of winning from spotlight but just to get a clear second opinion I have gone to the Timeform site as I am going to have a decent bet on this selection. Their summary of the horses chance today is.

4/1, career best when winning 11-runner minor event at this C&D 7 days ago by 2¾ lengths from Grandee Daisy. Big player under a penalty. **TIMEFIRM Analyst's Verdict**
ROCA MAGICA *was well adrift of Grandee Daisy over C&D on her penultimate start but proved that run all wrong when decisively outpointing Michael Appleby's charge back here last week. She is taken to confirm her superiority over that rival, despite the terms being less favourable on this occasion. Each-way cases can be made for Cristal Pallas Cat, Crazy Spin and Loose Chippings.*

To back this up further I have watched a replay of the horses last run which I will always do before striking a bet. For the extra time it will take you to do this it is imperative. Do this at the Racing Post race card and click on the horses name, this will then take you through to the form page then click on the RED TRIANGLE

▶ 13Feb20   Cfd C6 3K   1m   St   9-0   1/11 by 2¾L Grandee Daisy 9-5   4/1F   R Havlin   47   43   **55**

There you have the basic selection method, the one where selections listed in the results page (tables in the end pages of the book) are all shown as being backed to one point level stakes to BSP (betfair SP)

THE THEORY

It is obvious that a jockey will go to ride at a course for a trainer who provides him with plenty of winners at the track. But most of the top jockeys have retainers with top stables as they get paid by the trainers owners to ride their horses and they have first call on the jockeys services. Top jockeys will try to get jobs with the best yards as they are likely to provide them with plenty of winners throughout the year and hopefully have some promising inmates that may supply the jockey with some mounts in prestige races such as Group races, Listed races etc. It is also a positive for a stable to have a very good retained jockey as this attracts good owners who will pay for a better quality of horse, who wouldn't want their horse to be ridden by the likes of Frankie Dettori on the flat or Richard Johnson over the jumps? A top jockey is literally worth their weight in gold as they will generally give a horse the best chance of winning, bar accidents or mistakes which they make less of than other jockeys and certainly jockeys learning their craft in the saddle i.e. apprentice jockeys. Their analysis of the horse run after the race and where it should be placed in its future races is also invaluable to a trainer, believe me real good jockeys are few and far between. It is a long hard slog for a jockey who has proved himself or herself to be a very good apprentice to make it right to the top, it's a case of once they lose their allowance and have to compete on level terms with the top boys, it becomes very difficult. If you had prepared a horse to land a gamble or to win a top prize, would you book a jockey who had just lost their claim or a proven top rider at the track, who is a brilliant tactician and a proven winner without the aid of a claim?

To prove the case my top six jockeys riding on the flat turf are Ryan Moore - Retained by top Irish trainer Aiden O'Brien, William Buick and James Doyle- both retained by owners Godolphin who's trainers are Saeed Bin Suroor and Charlie Appleby, Frankie Dettori - retained by John Gosden, Jim Crowley - retained by owner Hamdan Al Maktoumand Oisin Murphy the newly crowned young champion jockey who has a terrific future ahead of him - retained by Qatar racing, all top class operations who own the best horses and breeding stock who will all be aiming for the top prizes on the turf in the coming season. Of course there are other jockeys that I like and trust in this sphere not included in this list.

All - weather racing is totally different to flat turf racing and the two jockeys who have dominated in this sphere and have been head and shoulders above the rest are Luke Morris and Adam Kirby who I would back all day long on the right horse. But do watch out for Ben Curtis who I have had many a bet on this winter in lots of races where he has done me a favour by riding lots of winners. He certainly seems to have the knack of being in the right place and no doubt the new all - weather champion if not turf champion at some stage in the future. A top job definitely awaits him.

Over Jumps Richard Johnson- retained by Philip Hobbs and top northern rider Brian Hughes - retained by Donald McCain are the two jockeys I really like along with up and coming young rider Harry Cobden - retained by top trainer Paul Nicholls, not far behind but still looks to have a few rough edges knocking off him before he becomes the finished article. How could you go wrong following such an esteemed bunch of jockeys?

This method does however throw some names into the mix that I wouldn't generally consider but their course records make them irresistible combinations therefore good value bets at some of the lesser tracks, such as Tom Cannon at Plumpton. He's done me lots of favours riding big priced winners generally for up and coming trainer Chris Gordon, neither really household names and that is why some of their runners go unbacked at this course as you will see from the full results

What is true about all of the above on this list apart from the younger jockeys mentioned is of course longevity. It has taken these guys years to get to the top and to learn their trade but once their talents are recognised by everyone in the game they stay there for a very, very long time.

Below is just a small extract from Champion Jockey over the jumps Richard Johnson's mounts in the past few days. This jockey has had a long association with his retained yard of Philip Hobbs who has stated while ever the jockey is riding he will use him(loyalty not being a great attribute for many owners and trainers) and that he will be retained by the stable while the jockey still has the desire to ride.

TOP JOCKEY

DATE	COURSE / CONDITIONS / PRIZE	POS.	FINISHING DIST / HORSE / WEIGHT / HDGR	SP	TRAINER
30Dec19	Tau 2m3fSft C4NvH 5K	3/14	btn 1½L, Fitzroy 10-12 h	16/1	O Murphy
30Dec19	Tau 2m½fSft C43yH 5K	2/12	btn 2¼L, Zoffee 10-12	8/11F	P Hobbs
29Dec19	Don 2m½fGS C4HcH 4K	11/11	btn 64L, Christopher Robin 11-7	16/1	T Lacey
29Dec19	Don 3mGS C3HcCh 7K	PU/9	Spider's Bite 11-5	7/1	H Daly
29Dec19	Don 2m4½fGS C1ChLM 42K	3/7	btn 1½L, La Bague Au Roi 11-1	9/4F	W Greatrex
29Dec19	Don 3m½fGS C3HcH 6K	5/8	btn 31L, Gangster 11-8 p	28/1	W Greatrex
28Dec19	Nby 2m6½fSft C3NvHcCh 7K	2/11	btn 9L, Tidal Flow 11-8 p	5/2F	P Hobbs
28Dec19	Nby 2m4½fSft C1NvHG1 26K	1/5	by 1½L, Thyme Hill 11-7	4/6F	P Hobbs
28Dec19	Nby 3m2fSft C3HcCh 12K	6/10	btn 36L, Strong Pursuit 11-12	10/1	P Hobbs
28Dec19	Nby 2m4½fSft C2HcH 11K	1/12	by 1¾L, Dorking Boy 10-2 ht	13/2	T Lacey
28Dec19	Nby 2m½fSft C3HcHM 6K	1/12	by nk, Fair Kate 10-10 t	8/1	T Lacey
27Dec19	Chp 2mHy C4NHF 4K	3/7	btn 13L, Java Point 11-0	5/2F	K Bailey
27Dec19	Chp 2m7½fHy C3NvHcCh 7K	5/6	btn 26L, Samburu Shujaa 11-6	3/1	P Hobbs
27Dec19	Chp 2m7½fHy C2HcH 13K	5/11	btn 22L, Perfect Man 10-11 tp	7/1	O Murphy
27Dec19	Chp 2m3½fHy C2HcCh 17K	2/7	btn 3¾L, Springtown Lake 11-3	2/1	P Hobbs
27Dec19	Chp 2m3½fHy C4MdH 4K	4/15	btn 12L, Gosheven 11-0 t	8/1	P Hobbs
26Dec19	Fon 2m1½fHy C3HcH 6K	1/9	by 6L, Dostal Phil 11-12 h	15/8F	P Hobbs
26Dec19	Fon 2m2fHy C4HcCh 4K	PU/7	Sky Full Of Stars 11-10 p	7/1	C Gordon
26Dec19	Fon 2m1½fSft C43yMdH 4K	3/9	btn 27L, I Like Him 10-12 p	EvensF	Ali Stronge

Including the Philip Hobbs trained runners who he has to ride for and his record over the past few days reads L, L, W15/8, L, L, L, L, L, W8/1, W13/2, L, W4/6, L, L, L, L, L, L A very small profit of 2.04 points is achieved

Take out the Philip Hobbs trained runners and the picture looks slightly different

L, L, L, L, L W8/1, W13/2, L, L, L, L, L. A profit of 4.5 points is achieved but from less runners, so riding for their retained yards possibly long term will drain our profits, but fortunately for us their retained yards are not necessarily the ones that are mentioned in the jockey bookings tables or course top jockeys table, and if I was to go through each of the individuals chances from Johnsons mounts over the above period i.e. only backing the horses that were unexposed or well handicapped then this list could possibly be cut down even further. But the fact is that Richard Johnson will probably ride close to or above 200 winners from all of his mounts this season if keeping sound

SEASON	WINS	RUNS	%
2019-20	98	530	18
2018-19	200	979	20
2017-18	176	901	20
2016-17	189	1026	18

If you take a look at the above table you can see that this season totals show 98 winners so far (he has actually surpassed this in the last couple of days and is now on 101) but his previous three seasons show totals of 200, 176, 189 averaging 188 per year so a great source of winners. We would not however show a profit betting on all of his mounts to level stakes BUT being selective and only backing him at courses where he is the top jockey and only on unexposed or well handicapped runners would show a very different set of results. Our method of selection will hopefully make very clear, the jockeys to follow and the types of horses you should be betting on.

It does not really matter whether or not you know who a jockeys retained stable is. You will get to know this as you use this method, but is doesn't really matter as the selections are coming from the course top jockey riding for the trainer supplying him or her with the best win to ride ratio at the track, or the course top jockeys mount coming from the jockey bookings section, both to be found in the Racing Post paper version.

CURRENT TOP JUMP JOCKEYS TABLE FEBRUARY 2019 – 2020

BRITISH JUMP JOCKEYS CHAMPIONSHIP

● CONDITIONAL JOCKEY

POS	WINS-RIDES	%	JOCKEY AND LOWEST RIDING WEIGHT IN LAST 12 MONTHS	TRAINER GIVING MOST WINNERS	WINS-RIDES	%
1	128-631	20%	Brian Hughes 9-13	Donald McCain	39-204	19%
2	111-612	18%	Richard Johnson 10-0	Philip Hobbs	30-170	18%
3	90-522	17%	Sam Twiston-Davies 10-0	Nigel Twiston-Davies	44-215	20%
4	87-421	21%	Harry Skelton 10-0	Dan Skelton	84-406	21%
5	72-343	21%	Harry Cobden 10-0	Paul Nicholls	53-223	24%
6	71-367	19%	Aidan Coleman 10-0	Anthony Honeyball	16-46	35%
7	66-279	24%	Nico de Boinville 10-0	Nicky Henderson	57-206	28%
8	65-311	21%	Gavin Sheehan 10-0	Jamie Snowden	26-84	31%
9	60-403	15%	Adam Wedge 10-0	Evan Williams	33-215	15%
10	53-298	18%	● Jonjo O'Neill Jr 10-2	Jonjo O'Neill	36-171	21%

CURRENT TOP ALL WEATHER JOCKEYS TABLE FEBRUARY 2019 – 2020

JOCKEYS

Jockey	WINS-RIDES	%
Ben Curtis	90-416	22%
Luke Morris	55-475	12%
Hollie Doyle	51-308	17%
Jason Hart	36-206	17%
Jack Mitchell	34-183	19%
Adam Kirby	33-193	17%
Joe Fanning	31-176	18%
Richard Kingscote	30-197	15%

The merit of only backing top jockeys again is clear to see from the above tables, most of the above on the lists will be top course jockeys and it is obvious who is riding the majority of the winners, and by the way at the time of writing Richard Johnson is recovering from a broken arm but states he hasn't given up hopes of becoming champion jockey again. Get ready for a barrage of end of season winners supplied by his faithful owners and trainers to keep him champ!! We'll see!!

Before we can progress further you need to look at what we would regard as exposed runners and unexposed runners, this will be the only grey area of this selection method especially if you are a novice punter or new to the game, this is why the comments in the Racing Post and Timeform come in handy when trying to form an opinion on a horses chances and why video form is very important too

UNEXPOSED / EXPOSED RUNNERS

EXAMPLE OF TWO UNEXPOSED SELECTIONS

An exposed runner is one that is not hiding any secrets from us. The horse has gone through the maiden or novice route, been given a handicap mark then possibly won a few races in handicaps from a mark around the same as the one it is running from today. E.G. Say a horse has been allocated an initial handicap mark of 80 (flat turf rating) and it wins from this mark and is raised 7lbs up to a mark of 87. It fails to win from this new high mark and the handicapper is slow in lowering the horse as it is running into places from its new high mark. After 12 runs it has dropped back down to a mark of 80 its initial winning mark and wins again, it's pretty obvious that this mark of 80 looks like the ceiling of the horses ability and if it's mark creeps higher than 80 it is best left alone.

The class of the race too plays a part the winning mark of 80 may have been achieved in a pretty good race, say a class 3 handicap if the trainer aims the horse higher next time out say a class 2 race or even a listed event then you have to assume the horse may struggle raised in grade from a higher handicap mark too of 87. But if the trainer decided that the best way to get another win was to drop the horse in grade to a class 4 where the chances are it would be carrying top weight but giving weight to inferior rivals it has a chance to overcome its new mark of 87. Always check a horses last winning mark and class of race it can win.

Some horses may improve throughout their career and move up the ranks through handicaps into pattern races but these types of animals are rare. A horse will generally find its ceiling of ability (therefore become exposed) and that's how we can gauge its chance of winning today's race or not. Good horses will win a maiden at good tracks like Newmarket and then go on to compete in races of the highest grade e.g. 2000 guineas, Derby etc. It is rare that a horse will win a good maiden at Newmarket and be seen competing in handicap company after. Generally a trainer knows what he or she has on their hands and the ability a horse has from what it is showing at home and of course on breeding and most trainers will give their horses every chance of winning a race by running them in the correct grade. I can remember being at Pontefract one cold wet evening in May and a horse of Luca Cumani winning a low grade maiden there before going on to win that year's Derby, the price of the horse that night I think was 5/2 what a certainty that was in hindsight which of course is a wonderful thing in this game, but horses dropping in grade are a great source of winners

Of course racing is not so clinical and it is not so easy to pinpoint a horses ability to the pound or it would be an easy puzzle to solve, horses have preferences for different types of tracks, going preferences i.e. firm, heavy etc. distances they prefer to run over etc. which all has to be taken into consideration, but you are always taking a chance if you bet on a horse that is running from a higher mark in a race today than it has ever carried to victory before as you are expecting the horse to run a lifetime best to win the race. It doesn't matter if a horse has run twenty times or 100 times if its back down to a winning mark or below its last winning mark it is definitely worth a second look if its ridden by the course top jockey especially if he or her has ridden or won on the horse before and is running for a trainer the jockey has ridden plenty of winners for before.

I am also a bit of an ageist when it comes to betting on horses and would back an up and coming youngster against an older more exposed rival every time. Unexposed meaning exactly that, likely to improve and surpass what it has shown to date.

I am plugging one of my previous best selling books here, because you should take a deeper look into the Handicapping System used by the BHA who publish official ratings for each horse and you should also take a deeper look into the Racing Post Ratings therefore my **DOUBLE TOP** book priced at just £13.56 has everything you need to know about the handicapping system + RP ratings and is a terrific selection method to boot.

If you already own this book then refer back to the chapters that explains both ratings and how they work. It is essential to know this and how to use information in the context of this book. You can of course get this information online if you visit the BHA website and the Racing Post website or email them both and ask the question – how do you arrive at your ratings? Both will oblige with an answer as they did with me. You cannot know enough about this complex matter of handicapping, race classes and ratings.

Double Top: Horse Racing System
by Mr Anthony Gibson | 28 Jul 2019

☆☆☆☆☆ ˅ 8

Paperback
£13⁷²

Get it **Wednesday, Mar 18**
FREE Delivery by Amazon

Kindle Edition
£8⁰⁷ ~~£13.72~~

An example of this was a horse that fitted the bill perfectly on the 14th of September 2019. I had just had a run of six losers and feeling a little sorry for myself when I came across this little hidden gem.

The meeting in question was Chester

The course Top Jockey was Richard Kingscote

The Trainer supplying the jockey with the best win / runner ratio was his retained trainer Tom Dascombe

Trainer Tom Dascombe had four runners on the card, three ridden by Richard Kingscote but two of these were fully exposed and the other handicap debutant did not look to have the form to win this particular race even though it was unexposed. None of these runners were given strong positive comments by the racing post or by Timeform and after close visual scrutiny of their last runs none of Tom Dascombes runners were made a bet and he did not have a winner on the card that day so my theories worked.

TOP JOCKEY

CHESTER TOP JOCKEYS
Flat 2015+

WINS-RIDES		TRAINER SUPPLYING RIDES TODAY GIVING BEST COURSE RECORD	WINS-RIDES		£1 STAKE	COURSE RIDES ALL RIDES SINCE WIN
39-216	18% Richard Kingscote [5]	Tom Dascombe	25-145	17%	-25.96	3
17-113	15% David Probert [4]	Andrew Balding	13-75	17%	-32.91	21
13-98	13% Paul Hanagan [4]	Richard Fahey	8-73	11%	-22.90	0
9-28	32% Harry Bentley [4]	Ralph Beckett	4-11	36%	+29.75	2
7-25	28% Jack Mitchell [2]	Tom Clover	1-1	100%	+11.50	0
7-71	10% Connor Murtagh [2]	Richard Fahey	7-49	14%	-21.75	24
6-54	11% David Allan [5]	Tim Easterby	5-35	14%	-14.00	23
4-21	19% Lewis Edmunds [2]		0-0	0%	-0.50	6
4-31	13% Alistair Rawlinson [2]		0-0	0%	+24.50	1
4-33	12% Joe Fanning [4]	Mark Johnston	3-18	17%	-13.25	6
4-33	12% Jamie Gormley [1]	Iain Jardine	2-9	22%	-10.92	1
4-38	11% Jane Elliott [1]	Tom Dascombe	3-22	14%	-8.40	8
3-14	21% Robert Havlin [4]	John Gosden	2-5	40%	+11.33	0
3-29	10% Jamie Spencer [4]	David Simcock	0-1	0%	-3.00	8
2-68	3% Andrew Mullen [5]	Mark Walford	1-3	33%	-59.75	19
1-1	100% Seamus Cronin [1]		0-0	0%	+1.50	0
1-12	8% Shelley Birkett [1]	Eric Alston	1-2	50%	+5.00	4
0-14	0% Duran Fentiman [1]	Andrew Balding	0-1	0%	-14.00	14
0-14	0% Rowan Scott [2]	Nigel Tinkler	0-3	0%	-14.00	14
0-11	0% Charlie Bennett [1]	Hughie Morrison	0-3	0%	-11.00	11
0-10	0% Louis Steward [1]		0-0	0%	-10.00	10
0-5	0% Gavin Ashton [1]		0-0	0%	-5.00	5
0-3	0% Dylan Hogan [1]		0-0	0%	-3.00	3
0-2	0% Thomas Greatrex [3]	David Loughnane	0-1	0%	-2.00	2
0-1	0% Cieren Fallon [2]		0-0	0%	-1.00	1
0-0	0% Brendan Powell [1]		0-0	0%	0.00	0

Superior figure denotes runners today.

With the jockey not looking to have a chance of a winner from his retained yard we now move onto the jockey bookings table found in the SIGNPOSTS SECTION OF THE PAPER VERSION OF THE RACING POST.

CHESTER

6-20	30%	+£40.00	Thomas Greatrex/David Loughnane		Roseina's Voice 1.30; Baby Steps 3.50; Kaser 5.00
			2015+ 7-28 25% +£36.00		
3-8	38%	+£5.00	ⓒHarry Bentley/Ralph Beckett		Manuela De Vega 2.05
			2015+ ⓒ4-11 36% +£5.75		
2-6	33%	+£29.36	Duran Fentiman/Andrew Balding		Grace And Danger 2.05
7-25	28%	+£9.30	Louis Steward/Sir Michael Stoute		Sextant 2.05
2-2	100%	+£22.00	ⓒHarry Bentley/David Evans		Dark Optimist 3.15; Scofflaw 5.00
			6-24 25% +£23.25		
2-6	33%	+£15.50	Shelley Birkett/Eric Alston		Redrosezorro 3.50
2-5	40%	+£3.03	Jack Mitchell/Amy Murphy		Private Matter 3.50
2-4	50%	+£5.50	Richard Kingscote/Daniel Kubler		Involved 5.00
9-34	26%	+£40.50	Andrew Mullen/Mark Walford		Bit Of A Quirke 5.00

The only other mount that Richard Kingscote has at the course is a ride in the 5.00 for Daniel Kubler (the trainers only runner at the track) so we now need to look at the horses profile to see if it looks to have a chance in today's race

43

TOP JOCKEY

5.00 Thyme People Handicap (Class 4) [SKY]
RACE 7 Winner £6,727.76 (1m 2f 70y) 1m2½f

£12,800 guaranteed. For 6yo+ Rated 66-88 (also open to such horses rated 81 and 82; such horses rated 65 and below are also eligible – see Standard Conditions) Weights highest weight 9st 7lb Minimum Weight 8-7 Penalties after September 7th, each race won, 3yo 6lb, 4-6yo 5lb, 7yo+ 4lb. Jamih's Handicap Mark 80 Entries 36 pay £32. Penalty value 1st £5,727.76 2nd £2,002 3rd £1,000.40 4th £500.24 5th £500 6th £500 7th £500 8th £500 DRAW ADVANTAGE: MODERATE LOW

No	Form	Horse	Weight	Jockey
1	9/219-0	JAMIH 12 D1 F1 ch g Intello-Havnda (0) Tina Jackson² Peter Jeffers & Howard Thompson	4 9-7	¹Rowan Scott(3) (94)
2	4-55565	COTE D'AZUR 6 D3 F4 ch g Champs Elysees-Florenta (13) Les Eyre Billy Parker & Steven Parker	6 9-7	Lewis Edmunds (95)
3	2153/0-	MOST CELEBRATED (IRE) 348 S1 b g New Approach-Piatra Santa (2) Neil Mulholland Stephen & Gloria Seymour	w² 6 9-6	¹Brendan Powell (81)
4	3633746	ROGUE 10 S1 F2 b g Epaulette-Miskin Diamond (12) Alexandra Dunn Helium Racing Ltd	p4 9-6	¹Robert Havlin (92)
5	6311194	SCOFFLAW 11 S2 F1 C1 CD1 b g Foxwedge-Belle Des Ans (10) David Evans John Abbey & Emma Evans	v5 9-6	Harry Bentley (92)
6	-560165	MEDALLA DE ORO 26 D1 S2 F1 CD1 b g Teofilo-Nyarhini (1) Tom Clover The Rogues Galery Two	h5 9-6	Jack Mitchell (93)
7	5130704	CENTRAL CITY (IRE) 26 D2 S1 b g Kodiac-She Basic (14) Ian Williams Spencer Coomes	p4 9-5	¹Cieren Fallon(3) (95)
8	8544163	INDOMENEO 25 D1 S4 F2 b g Piccolo-Cherrycombe-Row (8) Richard Fahey Middleham Park Racing LX	4 9-2	Paul Hanagan (96)
9	421-38	INVOLVED 18⁰ b g³ Havana Gold-Trick Or Treat (5) Daniel Kubler Peter Onslow & Gary Middlebrook	4 9-1	Richard Kingscote (92)
10	-509533	GARDEN OASIS 18 D1 F1 b g Excelebration-Queen Arabella (6) Tim Easterby T A Scothern & Partner	4 9-1	David Allan (95)
11	3-47751	KASER (IRE) ¹⁵ b g Invincible Spirit-Lethal Quality (3) David Loughnane Lowe, Lewis And Hoyland	4 9-0	Thomas Greatrex(5) (93)
12	3422149	BIT OF A QUIRKE 41 D6 S1 F3 CD1 ch g Monsieur Bond-Silk (4) Mark Walford A Quirke & Mrs G B Walford	v6 8-13	Andrew Mullen (92)
13	7780560	TOP NOTCH TONTO (IRE) 6 S2 F2 ch g Thousand Words-Elite Hope (7) Brian Ellison Keith Brown	9 8-12	¹Alistair Rawlinson (94)
14	1197-04	SEVEN CLANS (IRE) 14 D1 S1 b g Cape Cross-Cherokee Rose (11) Neil Mulholland The Affordable (2) Partnership	b7 8-12	¹David Probert (84)

BETTING FORECAST: 9-2 Medalla de Oro, 6 Garden Oasis, Kaser, 7 Indomeneo, Scofflaw, 10 Bit Of A Quirke, Cote d'Azur, Involved, Rogue, 12 Seven Clans, 14 Central City, 20 Top Notch Tonto, 33 Jamih, Most Celebrated.

The race is a handicap and our possible selection is no9 in the race Involved its form figures for its last 5 runs 421-38 (only run five times, only twice in handicaps) <u>Totally unexposed in this sphere</u>

44

TOP JOCKEY

```
Involved                                    9-1
4-y-o b g Havana Gold - Trick Or Treat (Lomitas)
Daniel Kubler              Richard Kingscote
Placings: 421-38                        Draw: 5
OR74         Starts  1st  2nd  3rd  Win & Pl
All Flat races......  5    1    1    1   £5,670
     12/18  Wolv  1m½f Cls5 Auct 3-6yo stand (AW)C3, 105
Stand 1-0-4 Std-Slw 0-0-1 Class 4 0-0-1 Dist 0-0-1
LeftH 1-0-4 RightH 0-0-1 Jockey 0-0-1

9 Mar Kempton (AW) 1m4f Cls6 61-75 Hcap £3,752
8 ran  STD-SLW              Time 2m 34.45s (slw 5.15s)
1 Nylon Speed 5 9-7 1 ........David Probert¹ 11/4F
2 Dono Di Dio 4 8-13 ......Scott McCullagh (7)³ 5/1
3 Double Legend 4 8-6 b ...Martin Dwyer⁷ 100/30
8 INVOLVED 4 9-5 ............Robert Winston⁹ 6/1
   steadied start, took keen hold, in touch in
   midfield on outer, ridden and unable to quicken
   just over 2f out, lost place over 1f out, behind
   inside final furlong (jockey said colt stopped
   quickly)
      btn 22¾ lgths [rpm46 rs21 or74][op 8/1 tchd
   5/1]
Dist: ¾-nso-1⅝-1¾-2        RACE RPR: 83/81/67
NEXT RUN: First 3 w1 p1 u1 Also rans w0 p1 u2

26 Jan Chelmsford (AW) 1m2f Cls4 71-79 Hcap
                                         £5,175
6 ran  STAND                Time 2m 5.92s (slw 3.12s)
1 Dommersen 6 9-2 .......Ben Sanderson (5)⁵ 4/1
2 Derek Duval 5 9-7 tv¹ ......Daniel Muscutt⁴ 9/1
3 INVOLVED 4 9-1 ..........Richard Kingscote² 6/1
   raced in midfield, ridden along and every
   chance over 1f out, kept on one pace inside
   final furlong  btn 1½ lgths [rpm79 rs61 or74]
Dist: nk-1½-2-1¾-4         RACE RPR: 86/85/79
NEXT RUN: First 3 w0 p1 u1 Also rans w1 p0 u1

10 Dec 18 Wolverhampton (AW) 1m½f Cls6 Auct
                                   3-5yo £3,105
5 ran  STAND               Time 1m 49.18s (slw 4.18s)
1 INVOLVED 3 9-2 ..........Robert Winston⁶ 9/2
   chased leader, went upsides over 6f out, ridden
   to lead inside final furlong, ran on
   [rpm64 rs40]                         [op 4/1]
2 Kynance 3 8-11 ...........Martin Harley⁵ 4/1 1F
3 Viento de Condor 3 9-2 v¹ ...Jack Mitchell³ 14/1
Dist: 2½-1¾-10-62          RACE RPR: 64/54/56
NEXT RUN: First 3 w0 p0 u2 Also rans w0 p0 u1
```

Looking at the horses form it had won a maiden at Wolverhampton on the 10th of December, it then ran in a Class 4 handicap at Chelmsford finishing close up from a mark of 74 (ridden by Kingscote). The horse was then given a break so possibly needed the run when well beaten in a Class 5 handicap on a different surface at Kempton. I have to say the distance beaten a little off putting, but was stepping up in trip that day, again its mark was 74. Today it is running on turf from an unchanged mark of 74 with Kingscote back in the saddle and back down in trip closer to the distance it won over at Wolverhampton (many trainers may up their horses in trip over run them over too short a distance to get their handicap marks down) in any other sport it would be called cheating!!

The Racing Post verdict echo my sentiments after studying the form and watching its past races but Timeform give me more faith to make this a bet.

SPOTLIGHT

COMMENTS FROM THE RACING POST

Involved Won a five-runner Wolverhampton novice in December but was beaten 22l when last of eight in a Kempton handicap (1m4f, AW) when last seen in March; has his first run on turf following a gelding operation so has a few questions to answer back down in distance.

TIMEFORM

Winner of a Novice race at Wolverhampton in December but well beaten when stepped up in distance next time out at Kempton. Only had five starts so too early to write off on turf debut with Richard Kingscote an interesting booking for the yard.

As the horse has only run five times and is running from its initial handicap mark of 74 which it did finish close up from on its penultimate start. We have to excuse the horses last run after a break and up in distance. Today's turf surface is a total unknown, the horse has to be a bit of a speculative investment but sometimes this has to be the case if you are going to bag some of the big priced winners the top jockeys ride.

17:00 THYME PEOPLE HANDICAP (4)

1st 9. INVOLVED 16/1
2nd 5. SCOFFLAW 5/1
3rd 13. TOP NOTCH TONTO (IRE) 14/1

13 ran. NRs: ROGUE.

J: Richard Kingscote
T: Daniel Kubler

Pos (Draw)	Btn	Horse Name Pedigree	TFR	Tfig	Jockey Trainer	Age (Equip)	Wgt (OR)	ISP	BSP (Place)	Hi/Lo
1 (5)		9. INVOLVED	< >		Richard Kingscote Daniel Kubler	4	9-1 (74)	16/1	32 (8.8)	55/-

TOP JOCKEY

The horse got up on the line receiving a terrific ride from Richard Kingscote the course top jockey winning at a great SP of 16/1 but an even better betfair SP (our chosen betting medium) of 32.0

Another example of an unexposed winner at Wolverhampton

WOLVERHAMPTON TOP JOCKEYS
Flat 2015+

WINS-RIDES	JOCKEY	TRAINER SUPPLYING RIDES TODAY GIVING BEST COURSE RECORD	WINS-RIDES	%	ALL RIDES SINCE £1 STAKE	COURSE RIDES WIN
154-1252	12% Luke Morris	Michael Appleby	9-63	14%	-346.20	2
90-553	16% Richard Kingscote	Ralph Beckett	7-26	27%	-97.07	0
55-483	11% David Probert	Ronald Harris	10-77	13%	-23.52	57
49-404	12% P J McDonald	Stuart Williams	6-15	40%	-84.50	1
47-232	20% Robert Havlin	Steve Gollings	0-1	0%	-24.70	1
45-483	9% Shane Kelly	Richard Hughes	18-123	15%	-190.41	0
43-398	11% Franny Norton	Michael Wigham	2-16	13%	-127.50	5
36-371	10% Rob Hornby	Tony Carroll	0-1	0%	+66.96	9
32-410	8% Andrew Mullen		0-0	0%	-160.42	12
29-292	10% Ben Curtis	David Evans	4-19	21%	-36.63	4
29-378	8% Cam Hardie	Antony Brittain	19-203	9%	-99.59	4
28-204	14% Daniel Tudhope	Archie Watson	1-3	33%	-63.75	16
24-434	6% Liam Keniry	Sylvester Kirk	0-17	0%	-239.75	27
23-229	10% Alistair Rawlinson	Michael Appleby	17-172	10%	-78.62	4
21-194	11% Shane Gray		0-0	0%	-88.68	6
20-182	11% Daniel Muscutt	Alexandra Dunn	3-10	30%	-69.17	3
18-207	9% Nicola Currie	Jamie Osborne	7-52	13%	-66.04	23
17-171	10% Martin Dwyer	Ian Williams	0-1	0%	-22.75	49
15-108	14% Callum Rodriguez	Julie Camacho	0-4	0%	-6.17	0
15-150	10% Barry McHugh	Tim FitzGerald	1-13	8%	+10.38	5
14-147	10% Charles Bishop	Eve Johnson Houghton	5-27	19%	-48.29	34
13-92	14% Lewis Edmunds	Derek Shaw	0-5	0%	-15.77	31
13-276	5% Eoin Walsh	Brian Forsay	0-1	0%	-130.62	3
12-206	6% James Sullivan	Ruth Carr	4-81	5%	-81.25	16
10-71	14% Poppy Bridgwater	Bernard Llewellyn	1-1	100%	+7.50	0
10-79	13% Finley Marsh	Stella Barclay	0-1	0%	+64.75	1
10-112	9% Kieran Shoemark	Charles Hills	1-7	14%	-36.25	14
9-77	12% Thomas Greatrex	David Loughnane	4-23	17%	-19.15	1
7-91	8% Mitch Godwin	Harry Dunlop	0-1	0%	-45.59	12
6-80	8% Philip Prince	Milton Bradley	8-7	0%	-45.25	17
3-37	8% Elisha Whittington	Lisa Williamson	0-20	0%	-17.75	10
3-78	4% Darragh Keenan	John Ryan	1-10	10%	-33.00	50
2-23	9% Gavin Ashton	Lisa Williamson	1-10	10%	-4.00	0
2-26	8% Grace McEntee		0-0	0%	-19.40	1
0-16	0% Kate Leahy	Archie Watson	0-4	0%	-16.00	16
0-1	0% Siobhan Rutledge		0-0	0%	-1.00	1

Superior figure denotes runners today.

The top Jockey riding at Wolverhampton today is Luke Morris, the trainer supplying him with the best course record with wins to rides ratio is Mick Appleby.

WOLVERHAMPTON TOP TRAINERS

Flat 2015+	WINS-RUNS	%	£1 STAKE	2YO NON-HCP	2YO HCP	3YO NON-HCP	3YO HCP	4YO+	COURSE RUNS SINCE WIN
David Evans ²	85-685	12%	-95.22	5-82	7-55	7-58	20-152	46-338	0
Michael Appleby ⁵	63-610	10%	-173.37	1-5	1-14	1-47	8-86	52-458	0
Mark Loughnane ¹	57-651	9%	-161.64	1-43	8-11	1-56	8-107	47-434	8
Tony Carroll ⁴	50-488	10%	-117.42	1-15	8-10	1-12	11-50	37-392	0
Jamie Osborne ¹	44-359	12%	-157.38	7-64	5-31	4-52	12-95	16-117	24
Archie Watson ³	38-179	21%	-16.51	14-41	5-20	8-14	8-42	11-62	7
Stuart Williams ²	31-165	19%	-32.98	1-5	1-5	3-8	6-33	20-114	5
Ian Williams ²	36-275	11%	-92.56	8-4	0-0	2-23	1-45	27-203	1
Antony Brittain ³	29-310	9%	-29.75	8-5	1-2	2-10	2-30	24-263	1
Ed Walker ¹	27-148	18%	-34.61	1-22	4-8	6-27	8-52	8-39	2
Richard Hughes ¹	27-207	13%	-57.87	6-34	4-21	6-31	8-68	3-53	0
Sylvester Kirk ¹	26-228	11%	-55.99	2-36	2-19	3-16	6-76	13-81	7
David Loughnane ²	26-229	11%	+50.80	1-20	1-6	3-19	9-54	12-130	0
Ralph Beckett ¹	25-135	19%	-21.02	3-32	2-6	7-36	7-39	6-22	5

Mick Appleby is not the course top trainer

What is interesting here is that Luke Morris has seven rides at the track tonight but only the one mount for Appleby whom himself has five runners at the track. Is this the horse they think has the strongest chance of their five runners booking Morris to ride?

WOLVERHAMPTON (AW)

24-77	31%	+£23.06	Daniel Tudhope/Archie Watson	Urban Hero 4.50; Whisper Aloud 6.30
2-6	33%	+£6.00	ⓒRichard Kingscote/Mark Loughnane	Friday Fizz 5.25
2-8	25%	+£9.00	Darragh Keenan/Jane Chapple-Hyam	Bullington Boy 6.00
2-3	67%	+£7.25	ⓒRichard Kingscote/Stuart Williams	Restless Rose 6.30
			2015+ ⓒ3-8 38% +£6.25	
2-5	40%	+£7.00	ⓒP J McDonald/David Loughnane	Concierge 6.30
			2015+ ⓒ4-15 27% +£25.00	
3-7	43%	+£9.50	Ben Curtis/Michael Appleby	Zapper Cass 7.00; Doctor Jazz 8.30
6-15	40%	+£9.55	ⓒP J McDonald/Stuart Williams	Excellent George 7.00
4-15	27%	+£9.25	ⓒBen Curtis/David Evans	Brockey Rise 7.30; Pike Corner Cross 8.00
3-6	50%	+£5.88	ⓒLuke Morris/Ed Walker	Elena Osorio 8.00
			6-24 25% +£2.88	
3-10	30%	+£13.50	ⓒDaniel Muscutt/Alexandra Dunn	Born To Reason 8.00; Enmeshing 8.30
2-8	25%	+£13.50	P J McDonald/Alistair Whillans	Lyford 8.30

If we move onto the jockey bookings in the signpost section of the Racing post we can see that Luke Morris is on the list riding for Ed Walker in the 8.00 so the credentials of both horses must be checked out.

TOP JOCKEY

> **5.25** Ladbrokes Where The Nation Plays Fillies' Novice Stakes (Plus 10 Race) (Class 5)
> RACE 2 Winner £3,428.57 (7f 36y) 7f AW
>
> 10 — Plus 10 qualified
>
> 6538 **FRIDAY FIZZ** (IRE) bf 3 9-0
> 1 (3) b f Kodiac-Sugarhoneybaby Richard Kingscote
> Mark Loughnane Haven't A Pot & Lot Bellingbroke (66)
>
> **I LOVE YOU BABY** 3 9-0
> 2 (1) b f Cityscape-Ashtaroth Luke Morris
> Michael Appleby Craig & Laura Buckingham
>
> 773 **LORETTA** (IRE) 3 9-0
> 3 (5) b f Ithaq-Marlinka Callum Rodriguez
> Julie Camacho Elite Racing Club (74)
>
> **NICE FELLA** 3 9-0
> 4 (2) b f Kodiac-Across The Galaxy Mitch Godwin(3)
> Harry Dunlop Kingwood Stud Management Co Ltd
>
> 425 **QATAR QUEEN** (IRE) 70 3 9-0
> 5 (6) b f Kodiac-Alina ¹Daniel Muscutt
> James Fanshawe Qatar Racing Limited
>
> **WILDMOUNTAINTHYME** 3 9-0
> 6 (4) b f Doncaster Rover-Awaywithefairies Finley Marsh(3)
> Stella Barclay P J Metcalfe
>
> **BETTING FORECAST:** 4-5 Qatar Queen, 5-2 Loretta, 8 I Love You Baby, 9 Nice Fella, 16 Wildmountainthyme, 20 Friday Fizz.

I Love You Baby First foal; dam 1m winner (RPR 74), closely related to 6f AW winner Cottrell, half-sister to 1m2f winner Tom's Rock out of unraced sister to French 2,000 Guineas winner Ashkalani; makes her belated debut but yard is in good form and interesting to see how she figures in market.

The first mount of Luke Morris from our possible two qualifiers is I Love You Baby and as we are looking for unexposed or well handicapped horses only, you cannot really get more unexposed than this one who hasn't yet seen the track. Note the comments of the verdict in the Racing Post above which are very encouraging indeed for a newcomer.

I LOVE YOU BABY, bought for just £600 at Ascot in June, made a winning debut. She deserved it as she really stuck to her task in the straight but it's hard to know what the form is worth, as the runner-up probably needs a mile. The first two were clear of the rest.

1 (1)   2. I LOVE YOU BABY   Luke Morris   3   9-0   52.97   55/-
                              Michael Appleby   33/1 (12.35)

Luke Morris goes in on his first mount at unbelievable odds of 33/1 SP but 52.97 betfair SP this horse was a massive drifter on the day, when I looked at its SP before placing my bet with betfair the horse was about 7/1. Generally why the drift I don't know or care but almost 20 points bigger with betfair SP

TOP JOCKEY

The second mount for Luke Morris on the card although for a respected trainer has a totally exposed look

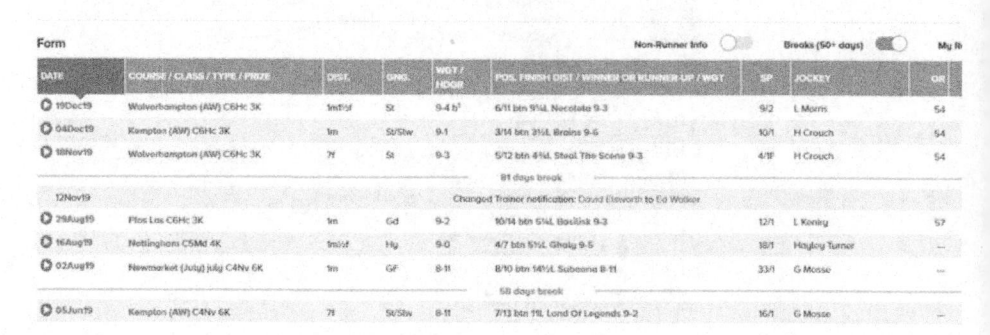

	784053 **ELENA OSORIO** (IRE) 15							b¹ 3 9-4	
	5	ch f Lope de Vega-Artwork Genie						¹Luke Morris	
	(7)	Ed Walker Peter Fagan						(65)	

Form   Non-Runner Info ⚪   Breaks (50+ days) ⚫   My R

DATE	COURSE / CLASS / TYPE / PRIZE	DIST.	GNG.	WGT / HDGR	POS. FINISH DIST / WINNER OR RUNNER-UP / WGT	SP	JOCKEY	OR
19Dec19	Wolverhampton (AW) C6Hc 3K	1m1f½f	St	9-4 b¹	6/11 btn 9¼L Necotaia 9-3	9/2	L Morris	54
04Dec19	Kempton (AW) C6Hc 3K	1m	St/Shw	9-1	3/14 btn 3½L Brains 9-6	10/1	H Crouch	54
18Nov19	Wolverhampton (AW) C6Hc 3K	7f	St	9-3	5/12 btn 4¾L Steal The Scene 9-3	4/1F	H Crouch	54
12Nov19					81 days break Changed Trainer notification: David Elsworth to Ed Walker			
29Aug19	Ptos Las C6Hc 3K	1m	Gd	9-2	10/14 btn 5¼L Basilisk 9-3	12/1	L Keniry	57
16Aug19	Nottingham C5Md 4K	1m½f	Hy	9-0	4/7 btn 5¼L Ghaiy 9-5	18/1	Hayley Turner	--
02Aug19	Newmarket (July) July C4Nv 6K	1m	GF	8-11	8/10 btn 14½L Subsonic 8-11	33/1	G Mosse	--
05Jun19					58 days break			
05Jun19	Kempton (AW) C4Nv 6K	7f	St/Shw	8-11	7/13 btn 11L Land Of Legends 9-2	16/1	G Mosse	--

The horse has run in three maidens without troubling the judge, then given a lowly handicap mark of 57 which was lowered to 54 and has been well beaten in each of these runs from that mark, not exactly screaming 'winner' so won't be carrying my money tonight

TOP JOCKEY

ADDITIONAL NOTABLE INFORMATION

Always pay close attention to any runner when it is ridden by the COMBINED FORCE of course top jockey and the course top trainer, see below that this is the case when Barry Geraghty teams up with Nicky Henderson at Cheltenham (not the festival meeting)

CHELTENHAM TOP JOCKEYS

Jumps 2015/16+

WINS-RIDES	%	JOCKEY	TRAINER SUPPLYING RIDES TODAY GIVING BEST COURSE RECORD	WINS-RIDES	%	ALL RIDES SINCE £1 STAKE	COURSE RIDES SINCE WIN
31-182	17%	Barry Geraghty [3]	Nicky Henderson	9-38	24%	-39.92	2
25-244	10%	Richard Johnson [3]	Philip Hobbs	10-114	9%	-81.11	8
23-116	20%	Nico de Boinville [2]	Nicky Henderson	18-91	20%	+60.74	1
19-172	11%	Aidan Coleman [1]	Dr Richard Newland	0-1	0%	-26.04	3
18-154	12%	Paddy Brennan [3]	Fergal O'Brien	13-83	16%	+4.25	0
17-120	14%	Harry Cobden [3]	Paul Nicholls	9-71	13%	+12.24	10
16-209	8%	Sam Twiston-Davies [4]	Nigel Twiston-Davies	8-77	10%	-52.84	0
15-144	10%	Harry Skelton [7]	Dan Skelton	14-137	10%	-51.29	4
12-157	8%	Tom Scudamore [3]	David Pipe	6-77	8%	-76.58	5

CHELTENHAM TOP TRAINERS

Jumps 2015/16+

TRAINER	WINS-RUNS	%	£1 STAKE	CHASES NON-HCP	CHASES HCP	HURDLES NON-HCP	HURDLES HCP	NHF	COURSE RUNS SINCE WIN
Nicky Henderson [9]	41-318	13%	-59.61	10-53	3-53	19-107	7-93	2-12	2
Paul Nicholls [3]	32-298	11%	-34.16	12-65	7-95	4-55	6-70	3-13	12
Colin Tizzard [2]	25-227	11%	-68.77	9-56	5-75	10-56	0-31	1-9	5
Nigel Twiston-Davies [5]	25-232	11%	-71.43	6-35	8-88	6-45	3-50	2-14	0
W P Mullins [1]	25-242	10%	-13.33	10-56	0-14	12-105	2-49	1-18	5
Fergal O'Brien [2]	20-142	14%	+44.25	1-9	7-43	3-33	5-33	4-24	0
Philip Hobbs [2]	18-196	9%	-84.22	3-23	5-68	5-22	3-68	2-15	9
Dan Skelton [8]	16-190	8%	-55.79	2-18	2-45	5-45	7-77	0-5	10
Alan King [5]	15-139	11%	-23.04	3-13	2-19	4-45	4-50	2-12	2

CHELTENHAM
●continued   SOFT, Good to Soft in places

scoop6   LEG 6

3.40 RACE 7   Park Mares' Handicap Hurdle (Class 2)   ITV4
Winner £18,768   (2m 4f 56y) 2m4½f New

21521/5 DAME DE COMPAGNIE (FR) 27 CD† h6 11-7

5 b.m Lucarno-Programmee Barry Geraghty

Nicky Henderson John P McManus (139)

BETTING FORECAST: 2 Dame de Compagnie, 6 Queens Cave, 9 Indefatigable, Lust For Glory, 10 Vision Du Puy, 11 Mega Yeats, 12 Misty Bloom, 14 River Arrow, 16 Carrolls Milan, The Cull Bank, 20 Liberty Bella, Shambra, 25 Dinos Benefit, Midnightreferendum, 33 bar.

Dame de Compagnie Won 2m4f Listed novice race here (2m4f) against her own sex in April 2018; not seen again until creditable fifth of 14 in major 2m handicap here (soft) four weeks ago, passing rivals on the run-in as if a step back up in trip would suit; player off same mark.

Dame de Compagnie 11-7

6-y-o b.m Lucarno - Programmee (Kahyasi)
Nicky Henderson Barry Geraghty
Placings: 1/322/1521/5

OR**132**	Starts	1st	2nd	3rd	Win & Pl
Hurdles	6	2	2	–	£34,041
All Jumps races	9	3	3	1	£43,710

4/18 Chel 2m½f Cls1 Nov List Hdl good (M) £14,238
11/17 Uttx 2m Cls4 Mdn Hdl good (M) £3,249
4/16 Lrsy 1m4f NHF 3yo £3,676
Total win prize-money £21,163

Good 2-0-2 Gd-Sft 0-1-1 Soft 0-1-4 V Soft 0-1-1
Class 2 0-1-1 Course 1-0-3 Dist 1-1-2 LeftH 2-1-5
RightH 0-1-1 Hood 1-1-4 Jockey 2-1-5

17 Nov Cheltenham 2m½f Old Cls1 Gd3 123-149 Hdl Hcap £56,270
14 ran SOFT   7hdls   Time 4m 10.64s (slw 19.64s)
1 Harambe 6 11-0 .... Tom Bellamy 16/1
2 Gumball 5 11-5 h .... Ben Jones (5) 9/1
3 Monsieur Lecoq 5 11-5 .... Lizzie Kelly (3) 9/1
5 **DAME DE COMPAGNIE** 6 10-9 h ....
.... Barry Geraghty 6/1
mid-division, headway after 3rd, outpaced after 3 out, stayed on again from last
btn 5¾ lgths [RPR129 TS109 OR132] [op 7/1]
Dist: nk-nk-1¼-4-3½ RACE RPR: 139/150/146+
NEXT RUN: First 3 w0 p0 u0 Also rans w0 p0 u2

19 Apr 18 Cheltenham 2m4½f New Cls1 Nov List Hdl (M) £14,238
9 ran GOOD   10hdls   Time 4m 56.70s (slw 9.70s)
1 **DAME DE COMPAGNIE** 5 11-0 h ....
.... Barry Geraghty 13/8F
settled towards rear, steady progress before 3 out, driven approaching last where not fluent, wore down leader 150yds out and in command final 100yds
[RPR130 TS94 OR134] [op 11/8 tchd 7/4]
2 Just Janice 6 11-5 .... Noel Fehily 8/1
3 Banjo Girl 6 11-0 .... Daryl Jacob 6/1
Dist: 1½-1-2¼-2-14 RACE RPR: 130+/132/126
NEXT RUN: First 3 w0 p1 u1 Also rans w1 p0 u1

TOP JOCKEY

Note this horse has the top jockey/trainer combination at the track and is also taking a drop in grade having run in class 1 events on her last three outings, has more than enough ability to win this race and is a very strong bet for me today

DAME DE COMPAGNIE, who finished to really good effect when fifth in the Greatwood on reappearance, relished the return to 2m4f, travelling well and getting well on top from the last. She's a useful mare who her trainer is looking forward to sending over fences, but there could be a big handicap over hurdles in her first, with the Coral Cup the obvious race to aim at.

Pos	Btn	Horse Name / Pedigree	TFR	Tfig	Jockey / Trainer	Age (Equip)	Wgt (OR)	ISP	BSP (Place)
1		5. DAME DE COMPAGNIE (FR)			Barry Geraghty / Nicky Henderson	6 (h)	11-7 (132)	2/1f	3.74 (1.7)

The price of 3.74 on betfair for this runner was a fantastic return for a horse that I could not see getting beat if running to form

12.10 RACE 1 — British EBF "National Hunt" Novices' Hurdle (Qualifier) (Class 3)
Winner £9,384 (2m 179y) 2m1f New

4 U11- CHANTRY HOUSE (IRE) (7/86) D1 S1 5 10-12
br g Yeats-The Last Bank
Nicky Henderson² John P McManus **Barry Geraghty**

BETTING FORECAST: 4-5 Chantry House, 4 Glory And Fortune, 6 Stolen Silver, 10 Pileon, 12 Shang Tang, 16 Olly The Brave, 20 Pipesmoker, 25 Sheshoon Sonny.

Chantry House Bought for £295,000 soon after winning his Irish point and was an odds-on winner of a soft-ground bumper at Warwick in March, the form of which looks all the better now (runner-up 2-2 over hurdles); described as "a big horse of the highest calibre" by his trainer and no surprise were he to make a winning start over hurdles.

Chantry House 10-12
5-y-o br g Yeats - The Last Bank (Phardante)
Nicky Henderson   **Barry Geraghty**
Placings: U11-

	Starts	1st	2nd	3rd	Win & Pl
All Jumps races	1	1	–	–	£2,599
3/19 Wwck 2m Cls5 NHF 4-6yo soft					£2,599

Soft 1-0-1 Dist 1-0-1 LeftH 1-0-1 Jockey 1-0-1

10 Mar Warwick 2m   Cls5 NHF 4-6yo £2,599

11 ran SOFT   Time 4m 0.60s (slw 30.60s)
1 **CHANTRY HOUSE** 5 11-2 Barry Geraghty 8/13F
   midfield and going well, effort 2f out, pushed
   ahead well over 1f out, stayed on stoutly,
   decisive winner [RPR124 TS41][op 1/2 tchd 4/6]
2 Edwardstone 5 11-2 ....Wayne Hutchinson 3/1
3 Shan Blue 5 11-2 ....Harry Skelton 6/1
Dist: 3½-¾-1¼-6-1¼ RACE RPR: 124+/118+/116
NEXT RUN: First 3 w1 p1 u0 Also rans w0 p3 u4

9 Dec 18 Tattersalls Farm (PTP) 3m   Open Mdn
15 ran YIELD   Time 6m 11.00s
1 **CHANTRY HOUSE** 4 11-11 ....J J Codd 3/1
   rr of mid div, 8th 5out, gd prog frm 4out, disp
   3out, ld bef last, sow close home [RPR94]
2 Envol Pierji 4 11-11 ....F Maguire 6/4F
3 Cuff Parade 4 11-11 ....C M Smith 8/1
Dist: ¾-12-20-2-2   RACE RPR: 94/93/81
NEXT RUN: First 3 w1 p1 u1 Also rans w2 p2 u8

29 Apr 18 Stowlin (PTP) 3m   Open Mdn
14 ran YIELD   Time 6m 21.00s
1 Monkfish 4 11-6 ....P J Cawley (5) 6/1
2 Gameface 4 11-11 ....J P O'Rourke 4/1
3 Opposites Attract 4 11-11 ....M J O'Hare 10/1
U **CHANTRY HOUSE** 4 11-11 ....A J Fox 6/1
   pr, ld aftr 5th, qcknd well aftr 4out, bd mstk & ur
   when in front 3out
Dist: ½-1½-3-12   RACE RPR: 91/90/88
●NEXT RUN: First 3 w0 p2 u1 Also rans w2 p4 u5

You are always taking a chance when backing a horse coming from National Hunt Flat races to hurdles as we don't really know how they are going to take to the hurdles, but a top yard will have their runners well schooled and this fellow jumped well on debut, his trainer Nicky Henderson had made no secret that he held this horse in high regard and even though the race looked pretty competitive the horse won well. The two selections ridden by the course top jockey Geraghty for course top trainer Henderson were both two very strong bets for me and made my weekend a very profitable one

ONE TRICK JOCKEYS

LINGFIELD TOP JOCKEYS

Jumps 2015/16+

WINS-RIDES		TRAINER SUPPLYING RIDES TODAY GIVING BEST COURSE RECORD	WINS-RIDES		ALL RIDES £1 STAKE	COURSE RIDES SINCE WIN
16-57	28% Leighton Aspell [1]	....	0-0	0%	+41.93	0
11-41	27% Gavin Sheehan [2]	Laura Young	0-1	0%	–0.58	0

Note the above: The top jockey riding at Lingfield today is Leighton Aspell who has no trainer mentioned in the trainer supplying rides today giving best course record wins- rides which is pretty unusual. He is also not listed in the jockey booking section so following our previous rules this jockey would not be a bet, but why has he gone to the track for just the one mount today? Further investigation is required as you cannot simply dismiss a course top jockey with just one the mount

2.05 RACE 4 — Watch Sky Sports Racing In HD SKY
Maiden Hurdle (Class 4)
Winner £3,768.84   2m3½f

£5,800 guaranteed For 4yo+ Weights: 4yo 10st 5lb; 5yo+ 11st 4lb Allowances fillies & mares 7lb, no allowance to take a horse's weight below 10st Entries 16 pay £29 Penalty value 1st £3,768.84 2nd £1,106.64 3rd £553.32 4th £276.66

1	009 ALFSBOY (IRE) 31 b g Shirocco-Full Of Spirit Nigel Twiston-Davies Carl Hinchy And Mark Scott	5 11-4	¹Jamie Bargary	(69)
2	2/ COHESION 812 (139f) b g Champs Elysees-Winter Bloom David Bridgwater Andrew Duffield	7 11-4	¹Brendan Powell	(121)
3	30 CRISTAL SPIRIT 16 b g Nathaniel-Celestial Girl Jim Boyle Reynolds Farm Syndicate	5 11-4	Leighton Aspell	(113)
4	4/43-54 ENZO D'AIRY (FR) 24 BF b g Ancillero-Persiana d'Airy Venetia Williams Dr Moira Hamlin	6 11-4	Charlie Deutsch	(126)
5	5/234 MICKEY BUCKMAN 36 b g Gleaming-Mywaywoway Gary Moore Mr & Mrs R Sage	7 11-4	Joshua Moore	(131)
6	14-6 A PERFECT GIFT (IRE) 72 51 br m Presenting-Kaynas Choice Olly Murphy M Lambert	w¹ 6 10-11	Richard Johnson	(124)
7	7 CONJURING TRICK 76 b m Great Pretender-Magic Score Charlie Longsdon The Queen	5 10-11	¹Aidan Coleman	(116)

BETTING FORECAST: 15-8 Mickey Buckman, 7-2 A Perfect Gift, 5 Cohesion, Enzo d'Airy, 7 Cristal Spirit, 8 Conjuring Trick, 40 Alfsboy.

Cristal Spirit Fair stayer on Flat, winning on heavy ground in October for George Baker; came from off pace when third of nine to a runaway winner in novice hurdle at Plumpton (2m, heavy) in December, 12 days before soundly beaten at Newbury (33-1); sights are lowered again and he needs a second look.

TOP JOCKEY

The horse is unexposed having only run twice over hurdles

[racing form for Cristal Spirit]

The horse has run in two class 4 novice hurdles and now steps down into a maiden hurdle.

[selection line: 1 — 3. CRISTAL SPIRIT — Leighton Aspell / Jim Boyle — 5 — 11-4 — 12/1 — 15.27 (6.4) — 80/-]

The horse was certainly worth a second look and it won at terrific odds of 12/1SP and 15.27 betfair SP note here too that the trainer had only the one runner at the track, but this trainer does not have many runners over jumps and is better known for his flat racing exploits which does make the selection look even more appealing.

Another example of this occurred with Jockey Ben Curtis on the 03/03/20

SOUTHWELL (AW) TOP JOCKEYS
Flat 2016+

WINS-RIDES		TRAINER SUPPLYING RIDES TODAY GIVING BEST COURSE RECORD	WINS-RIDES	%	ALL RIDES SINCE £1 STAKE	COURSE RIDES WIN
55-290	19% Ben Curtis [1]		0-0	0%	+33.81	8
48-437	11% Luke Morris [3]	Michael Appleby	8-85	9%	-178.04	2
37-331	11% Andrew Mullen [2]	Michael Attwater	2-7	29%	-92.07	6
35-244	14% Alistair Rawlinson [3]	Michael Appleby	34-206	17%	-61.35	22

TOP JOCKEY

As you can see above Ben Curtis is the top jockey riding at South well and has only the one mount but again no named trainer.

1 (10)		4. GOING NATIVE		Ben Curtis Olly Williams	5 (b)	9-5 (53)	4/5f	1.8 (1.17)

As you can see the horse won and was very strongly fancied 4/5 favourite, 1.8 betfair it was the trainers only runner at the track. The horse had won its previous race in facile style from a mark of 49 and today was running off 53 just 4lbs higher which looked extremely fair having watched the horse win on the bridle on the Racing post website on its previous run over course and distance, pretty obvious why Curtis had gone for just this one mount at the track and another successful big bet struck.

ONE TRICK TRAINERS

Something that should be noted by all users of this method as these selections are absolute **GOLD DUST** and if you only followed these types of runners along with the one trick jockeys you have a very selective / profitable method indeed.

Below is an example of a course Top Jockey, in this case Ben Curtis riding at Newcastle for Newmarket trainer William Haggas I have added an addition screenshot here of the course trainers which again can be found in the Signpost Section of the Racing Post paper version. When a trainer has just one runner at a course and has booked the top course jockey this scenario is definitely one to note, especially if the trainer has a terrific strike rate at the course which William Haggas definitely has. He shows a 35% strike with all of his runners here to date. Not only that if you look at the Top Jockeys table when the two combine they uphold this strike rate, not only that they show a fantastic level stakes profit at the track of +22.75. when I was going through this data on Saturday morning you could say that I was getting quite excited about this selections chances of winning.

●FORM p73   NEXT RACE 5.00 Haydock RTV p43

NEWCASTLE (AW) TOP JOCKEYS
Flat 2016+

WINS-RIDES		TRAINER SUPPLYING RIDES TODAY GIVING BEST COURSE RECORD	WINS-RIDES		ALL RIDES £1 STAKE	COURSE RIDES SINCE WIN
72-419	17% Ben Curtis [6]	William Haggas	7-20	35%	+22.75	0
60-515	12% P J McDonald [4]	James Bethell	10-51	20%	−92.99	2
46-490	9% Andrew Mullen [2]	Ben Haslam	17-93	18%	−58.83	0
44-368	12% Luke Morris [2]	Charles Hills	2-6	33%	−115.41	0
41-233	18% Callum Rodriguez [3]	Michael Dods	12-54	22%	+75.31	2
31-375	8% Jason Hart [3]	Eric Alston	2-7	29%	−137.21	3
31-418	7% Paul Mulrennan [2]	Susan Corbett	2-14	14%	−187.07	1

Ben Curtis was our top jockey to follow at Newcastle this evening with 6 mounts.

The Trainer supplying him with the most winners to runners is William Haggas who has just the one runner up at the track this evening.

TOP JOCKEY

Jockey bookings

Significant jockey/trainer combinations, in profit to £1 bet;
BOLD data = current season only; LIGHT = last four seasons, plus current.
☒ = data is course specific
(therefore **bold** data with ☒ = today's course, current season).
Flat season is defined as from January 1.
Includes those with more than one win, a strike-rate of at least 25% and a level-stakes profit.

NEWCASTLE (AW)

2-7	29%	+£7.50	☒Lewis Edmunds/Les Eyre	Cote D'Azur 6.00; Olivia R 8.30
2-5	40%	+£6.00	James Sullivan/Roger Fell	Muntadab 6.00
3-12	25%	+£10.25	☒Cam Hardie/Antony Brittain	Tathmeen 6.30; One One Seven 8.30
2-3	67%	+£12.75	Jason Hart/Eric Alston	Spirit Power 6.30
2-2	100%	+£10.75	☒Harry Russell/Antony Brittain	Mutabaahy 6.30; Lucky Lodge 8.00
7-20	35%	+£6.73	☒Ben Curtis/William Haggas	Manaabit 7.00
			2016+ 29-85 34% +£25.71	
2-6	33%	+£9.00	☒Faye McManoman/Nigel Tinkler	Tele Coed 7.00
2-6	33%	+£7.00	☒Luke Morris/Charles Hills	Quiet Night 7.00
2-8	25%	+£5.50	☒Jason Hart/Julie Camacho	I Know How 8.00; Dream Mount 8.30

Checking the Jockey bookings table we can see that Ben Curtis is not booked to ride for any other trainers on this list so our only bet at the track tonight will be for our One Trick Trainer William Haggas.

The Additional screenshot which I do look at shows that William Haggas has a terrific strike rate at the course of 35% and you can see that this 35% strike rate is matched when the Jockey / trainer combine at the track. They also show a very healthy profit of +£22.75 to a £1 level stake.

Course trainers

● TRAINERS with best wins-runs % from at least three course wins

Trainer	Course	Wins-Runs	%
Richard Hobson	Hayd	3-6	50%
William Haggas	Newc	31-89	35%
Paul Nicholls	Winc	98-287	34%
Charles Hills	Newc	16-64	25%
Nicky Henderson	Hayd	11-44	25%
Harry Fry	Hayd	4-16	25%
Roger Varian	Ling	29-120	24%
David Lanigan	Ling	8-34	24%
Tom Lacey	Winc	4-17	24%
Roger Varian	Newc	28-122	23%
Harry Fry	Asct	14-62	23%
Dr Richard Newland	Asct	7-30	23%
Nicky Henderson	Winc	8-37	22%
Kerry Lee	Hayd	4-18	22%
Nicky Henderson	Asct	32-154	21%
Mark Johnston	Ling	66-329	20%
Archie Watson	Ling	55-269	20%
Tom Dascombe	Ling	21-105	20%
Tom George	Hayd	9-44	20%
Anthony Honeyball	Asct	3-15	20%

TOP JOCKEY

```
7.00    Ladbrokes Home Of The Odds      SKY
RACE 5  Boost Fillies' Novice Stakes (Div I)
        (Class 5)
        Winner £3,428.57              (1m 5y)1m AW
```

£5,300 guaranteed For 3yo+ fillies & mares Weights 3yo 9st 9lb; 4yo+ 10st Penalties for each Auction or Median Auction race won 5lb; for each other race won 7lb (Sellers and Claimers excluded for the purposes of penalties) Entries 25 pay £26 Penalty values 1st £3,428.57 2nd £1,020.25 3rd £509.86 4th £254.93
DRAW ADVANTAGE: SLIGHT HIGH

		Horse		Weight
1 (11)		RED DRAGONESS (IRE) (420) ch f Dragon Pulse-Salydora Philip Kirby Roofing Consultants Group	¹Nick Barratt-Atkin(7)	4 10-0
2 (2)		6 BETUSHKA (IRE) 37 b f Archipenko-Wood Fairy Richard Fahey Mrs P B E P Farr	¹Paul Hanagan (85)	3 8-9
3 (8)		CHENILLE (IRE) b f Nathaniel-Comlin Lawrence Mullaney Geoff & Sandra Turnbull	Cam Hardie	3 8-9
4 (7)		DEFENCE GIRL (USA) b f First Defence-Supposition Simon Crisford Hussain Alabbas Lootah	P J McDonald	3 8-9
5 (1)		77- •LADY LATTE (IRE) 157 b f Anjaal-Cappuccino K R Burke Mo Charge & Mrs E Burke	Rhona Pindar(7) (56)	3 8-9
6 (3)		05 MANAABIT (IRE) 17 b f Kodiac-Pilates William Haggas Hamdan Al Maktoum	¹Ben Curtis (70)	3 8-9
7 (9)		0- QUIET NIGHT (IRE) 71 b f Dark Angel-Pindrop Charles Hills B W Hills	¹Luke Morris (40)	3 8-9
8 (5)		23-22 RIDESON 20 BF b f Golden Horn-Reledhur Roger Varian Sheikh Ahmed Al Maktoum	Jack Mitchell (85)	3 8-9
9 (10)		8- STAND FREE 81 b f Helmet-Ivory Silk Suzzanne France Miss Kate Dobb & Stuart Dobb	James Sullivan (80)	h 3 8-9
10 (4)		TELE COED b f Telescope-Discoed Nigel Tinkler Ms Sara Hattersley	Faye McManoman(5)	3 8-9
11 (6)		6- ZERE 129 b f Iffraaj-Ziniwu Archie Watson Nurlan Bizakov	¹Adam McNamara (93)	3 8-9

• LADY LATTE Engaged 2.15 Kempton Sunday

2019 (5 ran) Orchid Star (1) Charlie Appleby 3 9-0 1/12F   Daniel Tudhope RPR69

BETTING FORECAST: 11-10 Rideson, 100-30 Manaabit, 4 Defence Girl, 8 Betushka, 14 Zere, 20 Quiet Night, Red Dragoness, 33 Lady Latte, Tele Coed, 66 Chenille, 150 Stand Free.

Our possible selection has only run twice so is totally unexposed, I have watched video footage of its last two races. On its debut the horse looked clueless and was certainly not knocked about or given a hard time of things by the jockey (an observation of mine on the race backed up by Timeform comments on the race).The second run, the horse showed up well and stayed on in the closing stages, obviously learning from its first run so likely to improve again, this stiffer track at Newcastle looked to me exactly what the horse needed and another positive factor to take from its last run was that it looked a better race on paper than tonight's race even though it is the same grade but that was a mixed race and tonight's race is for fillies only.

TOP JOCKEY

Manaabit 8-9

3-y-o b f Kodiac (7.1f) – Pilates (Shamardal)
130,000gns Y; second foal; sister to 1m winner Rhydwyn (RPR 89); dam 7f/1m winner (79); half-sister to 5f 2yo Listed winner Knavesmire out of unraced half-sister to 6f Listed winner Splice (dam of Lowther winner Soar)

William Haggas   Ben Curtis

Placings: 05   Draw: 3
          Starts 1st 2nd 3rd   Win & Pl
All Flat races 2   –   –   –
Stand 0-0-1 Std-Slw 0-0-1 Class 5 0-0-2 Dist 0-0-1

29 Jan Kempton (AW) 1m   Cls5 Mdn 3yo £3,881
12 ran STD-SLW   Time 1m 40.89s (slw 4.82s)
1 Group One Power 3 9-5 ......Rob Hornby [10] 11/2
2 Endured 3 9-5 ....Daniel Muscutt 1 9/4F
3 Lady Sansa 3 9-0 ....Hollie Doyle [12] 7/1
5 MANAABIT 3 9-0 ....P J McDonald [6] 40/1
   led, soon headed and chased leaders, effort
   entering final 2f, kept on same pace and no
   impression inside final furlong
     btn 2¾ lgths [RPR64 TS42]   [op 25/1]
Dist: nk-1½-nse-½-2   RACE RPR: 75+/74+/85+
NEXT RUN: First 3 w0 p0 u0 Also rans w0 p0 u1

3 Jan Wolverhampton (AW) 7f   Cls5 (F) £3,429
10 ran STAND   Time 1m 30.96s (slw 4.96s)
1 NohsaB 3 8-10 ....Jack Mitchell [7] 15/8
2 Symbol Of Love 3 8-10 ....Shane Kelly [10] 7/4F
3 Allez Louise 3 8-10 ....Lewis Edmunds [8] 40/1
10 MANAABIT 3 8-7 ....Georgia Cox (3) [2] 6/1
   slowly into stride, ran green and always in rear,
   weakened over 2f out
     btn 21¾ lgths [RPR18]   [tchd 9/2 & 13/2]
Dist: nk-3½-¾-1½-3½   RACE RPR: 77+/76+/67
NEXT RUN: First 3 w0 p0 u0 Also rans w1 p0 u4

SP☼TLIGHT

Red Dragoness Has shown signs of ability in bumpers at Wetherby and here this winter; needs more but this well-connected filly is bred to be suited by this sort of trip on the Flat.

Betushka Unfancied 40-1 shot for her C&D debut so it was encouraging to see the way she worked herself into contention late on from off the pace; nicely bred and is open to a good deal of improvement.

Chenille 12th foal; winning siblings include Cheviot (5f-7.5f including AW 2yo; 109) and Bochart (UAE 6f-1m dirt; 106); dam 6f winning half-sister to classy Gossamer and Barathea; trainer doesn't target these races.

Defence Girl 100,000euros yearling; fifth foal; sister to 1m AW winner Aegeus (RPR 73), half-sister to 1m-1.35f winner Postulation (including at two/AW/US Grade 3); dam Group-placed 7f 2yo winner (106); trainer is 20%+ in maiden/novices on the AW; worth a good look in the market.

Lady Latte Has yet to figure at the business end in turf events at 6f and 1m and she broke out of the stalls on latest intended outing; looks best left until handicaps become an option.

Manaabit Achieved very little on 7f debut at Wolverhampton but had clearly learnt from the run and fared much better when fifth at Kempton recently (1m); hard to assess the form with newcomers in the first three places but a good chance she will come on again.

Spotlight verdict in the post summing up the horses chances and coming up with exactly the same conclusions I had, therefore the horse will be a bet tonight.

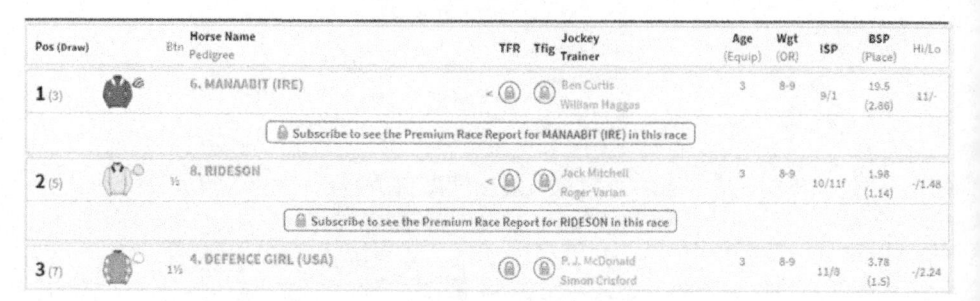

Pos (Draw)	Btn	Horse Name Pedigree	TFR	Tfig	Jockey Trainer	Age (Equip)	Wgt (OR)	ISP	BSP (Place)	Hi/Lo
1 (3)		6. MANAABIT (IRE)			Ben Curtis / William Haggas	3	8-9	9/1	19.5 (2.88)	11/-
		Subscribe to see the Premium Race Report for MANAABIT (IRE) in this race								
2 (5)	½	8. RIDESON			Jack Mitchell / Roger Varian	3	8-9	10/11f	1.98 (1.14)	-/1.48
		Subscribe to see the Premium Race Report for RIDESON in this race								
3 (7)	1½	4. DEFENCE GIRL (USA)			P. J. McDonald / Simon Crisford	3	8-9	11/8	3.78 (1.5)	-/2.24

The horse led from start to finish holding on well at the end and obviously enjoying this stiffer test. What was pleasing to see was the jockey breaking well and switching over to the stands rail straight from the off and dictating the pace as only a top jockey can do. Another weird thing about this result was when I looked at the prices Saturday morning, the horse was quoted 7/2 with most bookmakers. I do not bet with the online bookmakers, I use the exchange betfair and bet to betfair SP. When I logged onto my phone to watch the race I was shocked to see the horse trading around 21.0 on betfair just before the off so could not resist backing the horse again therefore doubling my stake as nothing had changed as far as I was concerned regarding the horse chances and to have the chance to back it at this price was crazy!! The horse won as I expected it to. I just could not believe my eyes regarding the starting price, what a result!! But I know there will be more big priced winners to come in the future.

Signposts

In the signpost section of the Racing post there is some very useful information regarding jockeys / trainers or both and it may just be worth a quick check to see if our top course jockeys are riding plenty of winners, although I obviously trust these jockeys to give any horse a good ride it is good to know they are full of confidence and riding on the crest of a wave, it isn't often these top jockeys go through baron spells but I can remember Ryan Moore having a tough time of things part way through last season and was riding as though he had lost his confidence, one way of checking is the list below where today possibly the only top jockey to appear on there is Richard Jonson.

Hot jockeys

● JOCKEYS with best wins-rides % from at least three wins in last 14 days, Flat & jumps

David Nolan	Wolv	3-7	43%
Cam Hardie	Wolv	9-23	39%
George Rooke	Chmt	8-21	38%
Richard Johnson	Ffos	5-18	28%
Tom Marquand	Chmt	7-29	24%
Tom Cannon	Ffos	5-21	24%
William Carson	Chmt	3-14	21%

Hot trainers

● TRAINERS with best wins-runs % from at least two wins in last 14 days, Flat & Jumps

David Pipe	5-13	38%
Nicky Richards	5-13	38%
N W Alexander	3-8	38%
Henry Daly	3-8	38%
Antony Brittain	5-14	36%
David Loughnane	3-9	33%
Tom George	2-6	33%
Eve Johnson Houghton	2-6	33%
Ben Haslam	3-10	30%
John Gosden	4-14	29%
John Gallagher	2-7	29%
Henry Oliver	2-7	29%
John Quinn	2-7	29%
Marco Botti	3-11	27%
David O'Meara	3-11	27%
Sandy Thomson	3-12	25%
Charlie Longsdon	2-8	25%

Again in the Signpost section of the Racing Post make a note of the which trainers are currently hot. I would rather be betting on a hot Trainer than one out of form. Also check the Journeyman Jockey section, sometimes a course top jockey will flit from course to course on the same day looking to ride more winners. Finally another good section although not crucial to this selection method, it is certainly worth noting the strike rate of our list of top course jockeys when riding for the trainers listed in the top course trainer section and the jockey booking section of the post.

TOP JOCKEY

Journeyman jockeys

- JOCKEYS booked to ride at more than one meeting
- Showing time of last ride at first meeting and earliest ride at next

Dylan Hogan ....Wolv 1.35-Chmt 5.25
Franny Norton ......Wolv 2.10-Chmt 6.30
Hayley Turner ....Wolv 2.10-Chmt 6.30
P J McDonald ....Wolv 2.45-Chmt 6.30
Hollie Doyle ....Wolv 3.20-Chmt 8.30
Luke Morris ....Wolv 3.20-Chmt 8.00

Trainers & jockeys

- TRAINER-JOCKEY combinations with best % from at least three course wins

Michael Wigham-Joe Fanning ......Newc 75%
all Newc; trainer 25%; jockey 14%

Nicky Richards-Brian Hughes Carl 57%
all Carl; trainer 25%; jockey 20%

Brian Ellison-Ben Curtis ....Sthl 43%
all Sthl; trainer 12%; jockey 19%

John Gosden-Robert Havlin Newc 41%
all Newc; trainer 36%; jockey 29%

Paul Nicholls-Harry Cobden Winc 39%
all Winc; trainer 34%; jockey 31%

Tim Easterby-Duran Fentiman Sthl 38%
all Sthl; trainer 22%; jockey 20%

Anthony Honeyball-Aidan Coleman ......Winc 33%
all Winc; trainer 17%; jockey 14%

Tony Carroll-Elisha Whittington ......Sthl 32%
all Sthl; trainer 16%; jockey 27%

Michael Appleby-Ben Curtis .Sthl 29%
all Sthl; trainer 13%; jockey 19%

Ivan Furtado-Jason Hart ....Sthl 29%
all Sthl; trainer 14%; jockey 12%

Michael Dods-Callum Rodriguez ......Newc 21%
all Newc; trainer 11%; jockey 17%

Alexandra Dunn-Adam Wedge ......Winc 21%
all Winc; trainer 9%; jockey 20%

Colin Tizzard-Harry Cobden Winc 20%
all Winc; trainer 13%; jockey 31%

Today the top jockey at Carlisle is Brian Hughes in the top trainer section it is Nicky Richards that supplies him with the most wins to rides and as you can see they have a very impressive 57% when they team up here.

Ben Curtis is top jockey at South well and Mick Appleby is the trainer highlighted in the top trainer section (29%) and Brian Ellison in the jockey booking section (43%).

Harry Cobden is the top jockey at Wincanton and Paul Nicholls is highlighted in both the top trainers section and jockey booking sections. He is also the top trainer at this track and when they team up they have an impressive 39% strike rate.

The remaining top jockey at Newcastle is PJ McDonald not mentioned in the above list.

The additional information is useful as it may influence the strength of bet you are going to place on a horse. The more positives you can gain from this information the more confident you can be about your selections chances without of course over cooking the selection method, a chance has to be taken at times about certain horses, these are likely to be the big priced winners you are looking to bet.

AYR TRAVELLERS' CHECK

THE following horses have travelled the farthest distance to Ayr

DRUMCONNOR LAD (IRE) (1.55) Adrian Paul Keatley, Rossmore Cottage, Co Kildare
AERO MAJESTIC (IRE) (4.15) & **DEMOCRATIC OATH (IRE)** (5.20) ....
....Gordon Elliott, Longwood, Co Meath
MIG DES TAILLONS (FR) (3.40) .... R A Curran, Downpatrick, Co Down
ISLAND MAHEE (IRE) (2.30) .... S R B Crawford, Larne, Co Antrim
JAMBOULET (IRE) (4.15) .... Charlie Longsdon, Over Norton, Oxon **324 miles**
THE CON MAN (IRE) (3.05) ...Donald McCain, Cholmondeley, Cheshire **217 miles**
SAM'S GUNNER (3.05)............ Michael Easterby, Sheriff Hutton, N Yorks **207 miles**
THEFLICKERINGLIGHT (IRE) (2.30), **WHOSHOTTHESHERIFF (IRE)** (3.05) &
MIDNIGHT LEGACY (IRE) (5.20) ....Philip Kirby, East Appleton, N Yorks **168 miles**
ROXBORO ROAD (IRE) (1.55) & **LASKADINE (FR)** (2.30) ....
....Ben Haslam, Middleham Moor, N Yorks **165 miles**
EMMA BEAG (IRE) (4.15) .... Julia Brooke, Middleham, N Yorks **165 miles**

Another section you may find useful is the Travellers check which is found in the race cards in the Racing Post. Any trainer that travels to a track is doing so for a reason especially if it's the only runner there and the course top jockey is booked.

MARKET MOVERS

I am a great believer in following horses that have been backed, especially winning jockey trainer combinations like the ones listed above. I know when I have owned horses in the past and the trainers have told me they are very well in themselves and expected a big run, if they looked to have a chance in the form book I would have a good bet on the horse and know many owners that are in the game just to land a gamble or two.

The site I prefer to look for market movers in the www.attheraces.com website look at each individual meeting listed on the day.

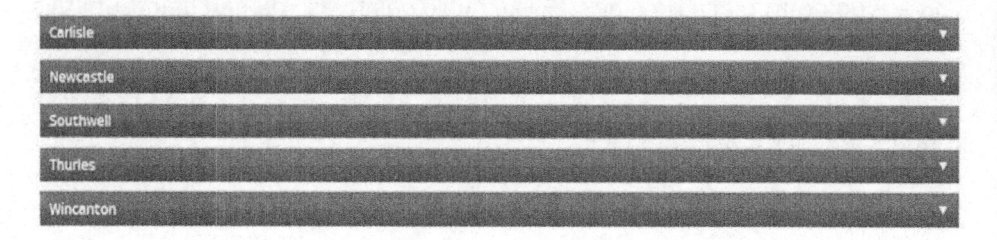

| Carlisle |
| Newcastle |
| Southwell |
| Thurles |
| Wincanton |

The best time to look I have found is around 9.30 am each day as the money is starting to come for the fancied horses around this time. Look at the evening meetings later in the afternoon (if you have time) for the later money coming in around mid-day. As I am writing this mid afternoon and the morning money has been placed. The Newcastle evening meeting is the next to concentrate on and it is interesting to see that Dark Heart in the 16.55 ridden by the course top jockey PJ McDonald for the trainer Mark Johnson who provides him with the best wins to rides ratio in the top trainers list has been backed from 1.38/1 early morning into 0.73/1 and again into 0.4/1. This horse absolutely bolted up as you would expect with so much confidence behind it. I of course backed it in the morning to betfair SP so had to take a bit of hit on the final price but even so a very easy winner and a confident selection

TOP JOCKEY

Newcastle
Top 10 Steamers for Newcastle

Horse Name	Race	Last Price	1st Show
Dark Heart	Ncs 16:55	0.4/1	0.73/1
Street Life	Ncs 17:30	1.63/1	2.75/1
Jonboy	Ncs 18:00	2.5/1	4.5/1
Mango Chutney	Ncs 19:00	3.5/1	6.5/1
Jeffrey Harris	Ncs 20:30	2.75/1	4/1
Betty Grable	Ncs 19:30	5/1	8/1
Got The T Shirt	Ncs 20:00	6.5/1	11/1
Hunters Step	Ncs 19:00	3.5/1	4.5/1
Primo's Comet	Ncs 18:00	8/1	12/1
Perfect Soldier	Ncs 19:00	12/1	20/1

BETFAIR V BOOKMAKERS

About ten years ago I wanted to back an odds on shot using my online telephone account which I had with one of the biggest bookmakers in the UK who have headquarters in Gibraltar so they can avoid paying taxes. I wanted £500 on this particular horse, I think the price was 4/6 to return me £335 profit. I generally don't like to bet so short but having seen the horses last run I just couldn't see it being beat and to be honest if the horse had been closer to even money or odds against I would have had more on it. After I had made my request I thought the guy on the other end of the phone seemed to be taking an awful long time to accept the bet and get back to confirm it had been placed. Luckily I had my betfair account open online so I placed the same amount on betfair to betfair SP, just before the tapes went up the guy from the bookmakers told me they couldn't accept the full £500 but would let me have £40 on. They had tried to use stalling tactics and then come back with this insulting offer of taking a £40 bet on a 4/6 shot!! To be honest they too knew this horse could not be beaten and didn't want to increase their liability on it. That was it, I closed all of my traditional bookmaker accounts and from that day on now only use betfair. When a big bookmaker is scared to take a £500 bet on a horse to pay out £335 then we are all in real trouble!! They had actually done me a massive favour and as I am sure you all know by now that using betfair you are guaranteeing yourself better odds so therefore better returns long term and unless you are betting £1000's a time you are also guaranteed to get your bet placed. I never take a price on a horse now, I simply let the selection run to betfair SP (BSP).

Take a bet running today as I am writing this. Fifteen minutes before the off I had logged into my betting account to place a bet on one of my main selection of the day Glorious Caesar (top jockey – trainer only one runner at the track) shown below highlighted in red showing at 8.2 on betfair and 8.0 with bet365. No advantage to be gained here using betfair, in fact you would be worse off if placing the bet at this moment in time as the bet with betfair is subject to commission so if it won would only return 6.84.

TOP JOCKEY

7 (4)	Calidus Mirabilis / Oisin Murphy	3.9 £283	3.95 £271	4 £251	SP
3 (7)	Believe In Love / Andrea Atzeni	4.8 £468	4.9 £110	5 £129	SP
5 (8)	Visibility / Tom Marquand	4.9 £189	5 £157	5.1 £286	SP
6 (1)	Lisbet / Kieran O'Neill	7.2 £201	7.4 £113	7.6 £117	SP
4 (5)	Glorious Caesar / Luke Morris	7.8 £185	8 £240	8.2 £134	SP
2 (3)	Goddess Of Fire / Darragh Keenan	11 £181	11.5 £94	12 £71	SP
1 (2)	Eventful / Adam Kirby	27 £2	28 £4	29 £15	SP

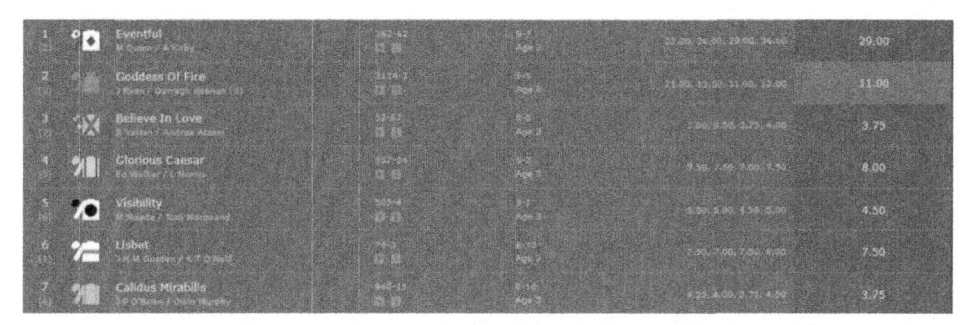

Pos	Horse				Result
1	Eventful				29.00
2	Goddess Of Fire				11.00
3	Believe In Love				3.75
4	Glorious Caesar				8.00
5	Visibility				4.50
6	Lisbet				7.50
7	Calidus Mirabilis				3.75

As the time progressed to the race starting. Goddess of Fire which funnily enough had been very well backed before the off was withdrawn as the horse would not go out onto the track, (this is why the final returns were shorter).

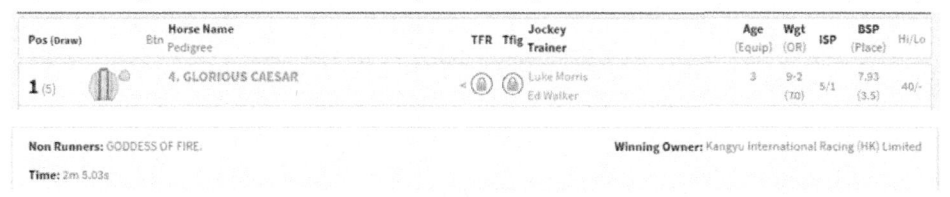

Pos (Draw)	Horse Name / Pedigree	TFR Tflg	Jockey / Trainer	Age (Equip)	Wgt (OR)	ISP	BSP (Place)	Hi/Lo
1 (5)	4. GLORIOUS CAESAR		Luke Morris / Ed Walker	3	9-2 (t0)	5/1	7.93 (3.5)	40/-

Non Runners: GODDESS OF FIRE. **Winning Owner:** Kangyu International Racing (HK) Limited
Time: 2m 5.03s

As you can see the selection won given an absolute peach of a ride by Luke Morris. I honestly believe no other jockey riding at the track would have won on this horse today, went for home at just the right time and held on well. The final BFSP 7.93 returned us +6.58 as opposed to the industry SP of 5/1 another gain of 1.58.

Another even better example of a horse that won recently for me was Manaabit running at an evening meeting at Newcastle on the all weather again ridden by the course top jockey Ben Curtis for William Haggas his only runner at the track that night.

TOP JOCKEY

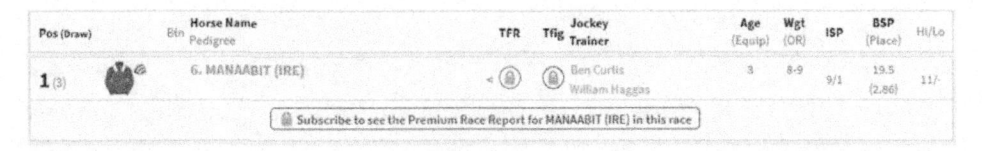

Pos (Draw)	Btn	Horse Name / Pedigree	TFR	Tflg	Jockey / Trainer	Age (Equip)	Wgt (OR)	ISP	BSP (Place)	Hi/Lo
1 (3)		6. MANAABIT (IRE)			Ben Curtis / William Haggas	3	8-9	9/1	19.5 (2.86)	11/-

Subscribe to see the Premium Race Report for MANAABIT (IRE) in this race

I backed the horse using BFSP on the Saturday morning around 11.00am. The horse was on the drift all day and returned a massive 19.5 to BFSP yet only 9/1 to the industry SP, a huge difference of +8.58 points when commission was taken off your betfair price. For long term backers this difference in price can cover most of the losing bets you are likely to strike using this method. Please, please follow my lead and use betfair starting prices.

BACKERS MINDSET

This part of the book is as important as the method itself because you can have the best selection method going but if you cannot show the discipline required to achieve the results I have shown then forget it. Again I make no apologies here by revisiting a book I wrote called Value Seeker which is still available on Amazon and an invaluable read, no point trying to re invent the wheel here.

Value Seeker: The Betting System
by Anthony Gibson
☆☆☆☆☆ ⌄ 57

Kindle Edition
£3⁹⁹ £7.99

Paperback
£7⁹⁹

Get it **Tomorrow, Feb 26**
Eligible for FREE UK Delivery
Only 9 left in stock (more on the way).
More buying choices
£1.01 (11 used & new offers)

THE PROFESSIONAL BETTOR'S MINDSET

When placing a bet I prefer to stick with what I know or think I know something about. I have followed the sport of horse racing for the past 50 years. If I had not learned a thing or two in this time then I think I would be residing in the poor house by now. British horse racing in particular gives me a bit of a chance of beating the bookies at their own game. It may seem to be a bit of an unfair playing field as the book is always calculated in their favour, but I like to pit my knowledge and experience against the bookie and consider it a fair challenge regardless of the one-sided book. And it's a challenge that I am up for as I only have to back horses that I fancy and only ones I consider to be value. If my methods don't produce a bet on any particular day, I don't try to force one just for the sake of having a bet.

Horse racing has so many fixtures these days and it is difficult to keep track of all aspects of the sport. The winning mentality or mindset of the horse betting professional is one of the hardest things to adopt, day in and day out, but it is critical if you are to achieve any level of success and, more importantly, make a consistent income from your betting on horse racing or other mediums. I truly believe that this is the one thing that sets the top one per cent of elite betting professionals apart from the other 99 per cent of mug punters and gamblers who aspire to make money from their <u>betting</u>.

It is possible to teach people the skills required to become a successful bettor, how to set up their betting bank, how to set their stakes, how to read form and make selections. All this can be learned. However, each one of us naturally has different levels of risk we are willing to take, a different level of loss we are comfortable with, different levels of patience and of course discipline to stick to our rules. We are all naturally different in our character and this makes up what I call our 'mindset'.

We can all learn the same skills but each of us will apply them slightly differently. I know this from personal experience through the activity of subscribers to my website and through emails I receive on a daily basis. Many subscribers come and go, yet my information makes long-term profits. It is simply because they are not prepared to put the correct bank in place,

stake my selections as advised, sit back and take the rough with the smooth and take a view to long-term profits. How simple is that? I can teach as many people as you like the same fundamental skills, even supply them all with the same daily selections and set them a level to start with their banks, yet each one will end up eventually with different totals in the bank. So how do we change our mindset? What is the mindset of the horse betting professional versus the punter?

The first thing we must do is look at the likely characteristics the horse betting professional has as his mindset.

Decisive – The first thing I always notice about the bettors who are successful, is how decisive they are in their betting. They make decisions and stick to them, whereas the average punter is unsure about things and constantly flitting from one system to the next, always changing his mind about the likely winner.

Patient – Professional bettors are also very patient and realise that they make profits month by month and season by season, not necessarily day by day or race by race. Most punters are quite the opposite, always trying to push things and chase their losses if they have a losing bet. They have a very short-term approach. I have a quote on my website 'get-rich-quick merchants not welcome'. Many of my mug punter friends have loads of money one day then are skint the next.

Emotionally Detached – By managing their money correctly the professionals do not worry about the outcome of each bet, but are quietly confident that month after month they will make money from the methods they apply. The punter who has little money management skills will always be worried about every bet. He will be staking more and more to try to make a profit and lose more and more chasing losses.

Disciplined – The professional always bets logically and rationally, each bet is well researched and will give him every chance of success. He knows that over time his selections will make him a profit. The punter will simply gamble making uninformed selections based on nothing more than irrational hunches or hearsay or on a gut feeling.

Bet within their means – Back to money management again. The pro always knows exactly what stake he is placing and why. He will always bet within the confines of his betting bank. The punter will be betting with money that is needed for other things, so becomes emotionally attached to it and the importance of the result.

Accepts Results With Equanimity – The professional bettor will not be the one jumping up and down at the side of the race track when his horse wins or cursing his luck if it loses but will leave that to the mug punters and gamblers who take everything personally. The professional knows tomorrow is another day and that the profits will come. He realises that in horse racing and betting your overall profits are what matter.

Now for a tip. Sit down for a few minutes and be honest with yourself – what are your strengths and what areas do you need to work on? You need to start forming the habits of success and create yourself a winning character when you bet. The person I have described above probably does not exist, as we all have our strengths and weaknesses and are all prone to making the odd error and mistake, that's what makes us human. But if you can take on board and adopt as many of the above attributes as possible then you are taking giant steps in the right direction. Photocopy this page, stick it on your computer monitor and refer to it on a daily basis.

Patience and Discipline – Above all else you must develop superb levels of patience and discipline to stick to your 'betting strategy'. This is so easy when you are on a winning streak and the profits are rolling into your betting bank, but what do you do when you are going through that long losing run? The run that lasts a week without a winning selection, when you know you have read the form and picked the best horse in the race and it still does not perform. This is when the true professional is disciplined and has faith in his strategy and ability. It is true that the longer you are involved in horse betting, the easier it gets, not just from what you learn, but more importantly because you have experienced the highs and the lows. You have had the good runs to see you through the bad runs. You know that you can weather the storm.

I am sure you are now beginning to realise that the life of a true horse racing betting professional is hard day's work day in day out, week after week. The professional is out there working hard, perfecting betting strategies and making slow, consistent profits. He will be building up his betting bank, increasing stakes and hopefully making a great income from his chosen sport, many days breaking even, many making a loss before the profits come in on the big days. Sometimes you may only have four to five of these days all month but these possibly bring in 90 per cent of your profits. However it is how you approach the remaining days that will set you apart as a winner or make you quit as another disillusioned punter who tried and failed. This is what sets the true professional apart from the remaining 99 per cent.

Hopefully the information in this book will help you considerably on your path to becoming a successful punter. I don't expect anyone to read this book then walk into their manager's office the following day and hand in their notice. There are many professional people making more money than myself from their chosen careers who have got there through sheer hard work and determination. I dread getting up some mornings just like the next person especially if I am on a losing run. I am not trying to promote the life of a professional gambler as the be all and end all, but betting can be fun, so let's try and make it as much fun as possible while also being profitable.

BANKING AND STAKING

Keep this simple, I generally back all selections to level stakes, and the results I have collated show the very impressive totals if you follow this rule. But I have to say that some selections do stand out as really good bets to me and the more you use this method the more you will get a feel for these selections that possibly warrant a higher stake than the normal especially ones where the top course jockey has gone to a meeting for just the one ride, or the jockey is riding for a trainer who has only sent one runner to the track or both the course top jockey and top trainer are teaming up at a track and again if they have only the one runner at the track. A trainer in good recent form is a massive plus as is a jockey in good form

I would suggest starting with a bank of just 40 points which is possibly excessive on the face of the results and losing runs to date, but I am a belts and braces man and would rather have too big a bank than too little where the latter gives you sleepless nights and nervous to pick a loser or to have losing sequences. A bigger bank gives you the confidence to ride the losing runs and eliminate those fears of losing, but remember that nothing in life is guaranteed and your bank may be lost over a period of time, so this bank must be made up of money that you have no other use for. The results shown are from the beginning of July 2019 to the end of February 2020. A full eight months is a long enough period. I would suggest to say this method is solid and should hopefully continue to perform well if used correctly.

DISCLAIMER

I cannot take responsibility for anyone losing money backing selections from this method. The method has been well researched and all results to date are 100% accurate. Do not act irresponsibly by chasing losses or betting larger than your initial bank allows

FINAL THOUGHTS

Some final thoughts on this method. Following top jockeys will bag you plenty of winners but will not necessarily make you a profit long term as you will see if you check the current jockeys table in the Racing Post. But taking a selective approach, therefore only backing the horses you really believe the jockeys can win on should pay dividends. Yes you will miss plenty of winners by doing so but this approach should produce a good long term profit if you use this information correctly. You have to take a chance from time to time by backing first time out runners or ones that haven't shown much form to date as they are unexposed, it is the unexposed runners where the bulk of your profits are going to come from and the ones that get me excited especially if I spot this type of runner that may have been given an easy time of things last time out or maybe run into trouble, this can only be picked up by watching re runs of past races.

Try to look at the whole picture and take on board the comments from the professional pundits working for the Racing Post and Timeform. This method is not black and white. I will possibly go for a horse you may not when we have weighed up the form or vice versa but you will back plenty of winners. Don't get disheartened when you hit a losing run, this is going to happen as you are likely to be backing lots of horses at decent prices along with plenty of favourites.

Try to weigh up a horses chances of winning once you have your final list of runners for the day but don't over think the method and talk yourself out of backing winners at long odds. These are the ones that are going to make the method profitable whereas the shorter bets should keep our bank ticking over and our confidence high. Have no doubts that top jockeys are in high demand. I can remember a trainer stating last season that there just isn't enough top jockeys to go around, there is no questioning this approach so stick with it through thick and thin. The statistics don't lie and these jockeys you are following are the ones that are riding most of the winners day in day out. Simply look at the jockey tables for the past few years

RESULTS TO DATE

Working from most recent back

Note: All selections shown are backed to one - point level stakes but I will personally vary my stakes one point being the least and upwards depending on how many positive factors I can derive from the information stated.

Results are from the 1/7/2019 to the 29/2/2020 a full 8 months

29/2	Superseded, **Clondaw Caitlin W3.48**, Black Pirate, Extrodinair	-0.64	+474.02
28/2	**First Flow W1.4**	+0.38	+474.66
27/2	Feel the Pinch, Ilhabela Fact, Dandys Gold, Away at Dawn	-4	+474.28
26/2	Riggs, Get on The Yager, Quart De Garde, **Fidelio Vallis W1.87**, Saintemilion, **Ask forGlory W1.26**, Mohareb, Sherpa Trail	-4.93	+478.28
25/2	**Glorious Caesar W7.93**, Agamemmon, Sweet Vinetta	+4.58	+483.21
24/2	Queen Aya, Fair Power	-2	+478.63
22/2	**Downtown Getaway W4.79**, Buzz, Bothwell Bridge, Toro Dorada	+0.60	+480.63
21/2	Scorched Earth, **Go Steady W3.9**, **Emmas Joy W2.8**, Ballycan Fame, Dark Heart, Moon Trouble, Discovery Island	-0.54	+480.03
20/2	Elton Des Mottes, Into the Breach, **Roca Magica W3.57**	+0.44	+480.57
19/2	Severano, **Lord of The Lodge W2.25**, King's Slipper	-0.81	+480.13
18/2	Luscifer, **Zapper Cass W1.1**	-0.90	+480.94
17/2	**Sao Maxence W1.56**, O'Hanranhan Bridge, Teescomponents Lad, **Bingo D'Olivate W2.71**, Malmesbury Abbey	-0.84	+481.84
16/2	Lexington Storm	-1	+482.68
15/2	Pipesmoker, **Manaabit W19.5**	+16.58	+483.68
14/2	**Three C's W3.15**, **Sandridge Lad W1.79**, **Luscifer W2.83**	+4.53	+467.10
13/2	**Garsman W3.93**, Poets Mind	+1.78	+462.57
12/2	Can't Stop Now, Divine Messenger	-2	+460.79
11/2	**Lua Da Mel W2.45**	+1.38	+462.79
10/2	The Tin Miner, Distant Goddess, Magnificia, Cat Royale, Superseded	-5	+461.41
8/2	Nube Negra	-1	+466.41
7/2	Global Society, Royal Ruby, Diamond River, Eesha Says, Elhafei, **Sandridge Lad W2.56 Gaelik Coast W5.92**, Mackenberg, Express Route	-0.84	+467.41
6/2	Tanqeeb, **Manning Estate W10.5**, Marada	+7.03	+468.25
5/2	Langer Dan, Glory of Paris, Gilka	-3	+461.22
4/2	Dolly's Dot, **Monbeg Zena W4.0**, Fresh New Dawn, Law of Peace	-0.15	+464.22
3/2	**Lily's Gem W3.35**, Feel Good Factor	+1.23	+464.37

TOP JOCKEY

2/2	Brewers Project	-1	+463.14
1/2	**Emmas Joy W2.03**, Midnight River, Beggarman, **All Yours W8.4**	+6.01	+464.14
31/1	Summit Like Herbie, **Subliminal W13.02, Matewan W2.3**, The Blame Game, Bring Upsun	+9.65	+458.13
30/1	**Keep Wondering W4.61, Worthy Farm W4.7, Calva Duage W1.67**	+7.58	+448.48
29/1	Kings Slipper, Rootless Tree, Catamaran Du Seuil	-3	+440.90
28/1	NO BETS		
27/1	Pres, Empire De Maulde, **The Con Man W2.16, Black Pirate W2.39**	+0.42	+443.90
26/1	**The King of May W6.4**, Snougar	+4.13	+443.48
25/1	**Corazon Espinada W4.3**, Agamemmon, Kitty Hall, Chidswell, **Neachells Bridge W4.87**	+3.81	+439.35
24/1	**Fantastic Ms Fox W7.88**, Chetan, Master Burbidge, **Griggy W3.0**	+6.44	+435.54
23/1	Young Offender, **Charmant W21.23**, Blowing Dixie, Sound Mixer	+16.22	+429.10
22/1	Minella Trump, Shine on Brendan	-2	+412.88
21/1	NO BETS		
20/1	Invincible Cave, **The Tin Miner 23.83**, My Boy Sepoy, High Maintenance	+18.69	+414.88
19/1	**Mayo Star W4.96, Glinger Flame W2.96, Prompting W1.44**	+6.04	+396.19
18/1	NO BETS		
17/1	NO BETS		
16/1	NO BETS		
15/1	**Bonds Lover W14.0, Shiskin W2.91**, Precious Cargo	+13.16	+390.15
14/1	NO BETS		
13/1	NO BETS		
12/1	NO BET		
11/1	Fraser Island, **Burrows Edge W6.39**	+4.12	+376.99
10/1	NO BETS		
9/1	**Double Martini W3.58, London Arch W3.27**, Limaro Prospect	+3.61	+372.87
8/1	**Kalooki W2.38**, Sound Mixer	+0.31	+369.26
7/1	NO BETS		
6/1	**Dunly W8.4, Castle Rushen W2.98**	+8.91	+368.95
5/1	NO BETS		
4/1	**Notforalongtime W2.2**	+1.14	+360.04
3/1	NO BETS		
2/1	Irish Acclaim	-1	+358.90
1/1	NO BETS		
31/12	**Wild About Oscar W3.8**, Emma's Joy	+1.67	+359.90
30/12	Port Of Mars, **Thyme Hill W1.73, Fair Kate W10.5**	+8.72	+358.23
29/12	NO BET		
28/12	Dubai Ways	-1	+349.51
27/12	Homer	-1	+350.51

79

TOP JOCKEY

26/12	Fusil Raffles, Vegas Blue	-2	+351.51
25/12	NO BETS		
24/12	NO BETS		
23/12	NO BETS		
22/12	NO BETS		
21/12	NO BETS		
20/12	NO BETS		
19/12	**I Love You Baby W52.97**, Lossiemouth	+48.37	+353.51
18/12	NO BETS		
17/12	Strong Glance, Maxed Out King	-2	+305.14
16/12	**Highway One O Two W3.37**	+2.25	+307.14
15/12	No BETS		
14/12	**Dame De Compagne W3.74**	+2.60	+304.89
13/12	**Chantry House W1.94**	+0.89	+302.29
12/12	NO BETS		
11/12	NO BETS		
10/12	**Tidal Flow W2.38**	+1.31	+301.40
9/12	**Just the Man W3.18**	+2.07	+300.09
8/12	NO BETS		
7/12	NO BETS		
6/12	**Nefyn Point W3.56, Minella Trump W1.82**	+3.23	+298.02
5/12	**Third Time Lucky W2.82**	+1.73	+294.79
4/12	Al Dowadiya	-1	+293.06
3/12	**Rajinsky W1.93**	+0.88	+294.06
2/12	NO BETS		
1/12	NO BETS		
30/11	Mr McGo	-1	+293.18
29/11	NO BETS		
28/11	**Air Horse One W2.72, Special Princess W3.12, Eritage W1.84**, Easyrun De Vassy	+3.44	+294.18
27/11	**Big Shark W2.56**	+1.48	+290.74
26/11	La Foglietta	-1	+289.26

TOP JOCKEY

25/11	**Hatcher W4.7, Colonize W6.31**	+8.56	+290.26
24/11	Idee De Garde	-1	+281.70
23/11	Echiquier, So Beloved	-2	+282.70
22/11	**Rivas Rob Roy W6.0**	+4.75	+284.70
21/11	Storm Rising, **Saint De Reve W2.59, Red Gunner W8.29**	+7.44	+279.95
20/11	NO BETS		
19/11	Black Tulip	-1	+272.51
18/11	**Go Whatever W3.01**	+1.91	+276.51
17/11	NO BETS		
16/11	**Bid Bad Bear W2.16**	+1.10	+274.60
15/11	**Very First Time W1.77**	+0.73	+273.50
14/11	**Chiti Balko W3.91,** Lord Springfield, Lady Bowes, TruckinAwaya	-0.24	+272.77
13/11	NO BETS		
12/11	Sofias Rock	-1	+273.01
11/11	**Windsor Avenue W2.28**	+1.22	+274.01
10/11	NO BETS		
9/11	**Give Me A Copper W7.6, Confiramtion Bias W4.42**	+9.52	+272.79
8/11	**Maire Branrigh W2.77**	+1.68	+263.27
7/11	The Bell Conductor, Notres Paris, Steele March, Floressa, **Diablo De Rouhet W3.0**	-2.1	+261.59
6/11	**Salamanca School W4.36, Dance Fever W5.5**	+7.47	+263.69
5/11	Sandy Boy, Thibaan	-2	+256.22
4/11	**Cuban Pete W8.66**	+7.28	+258.22
3/11	Whatmore	-1	+250.94
2/11	**Proschema W4.33, GartRockey W5.2**	+7.15	+251.94
1/11	**Langer Dan W5.6**	+4.37	+244.79
31/10	**Winter Getaway W6.2, Tomily W5.56**	+9.27	+240.42
30/10	**Bye Bye Lady W5.09,** Berkshire Filly, Presence of Mind	+1.89	+231.15
29/10	**Mighty Spirit W2.62,** Shadows Girl, **Filbert Street W7.68**	+6.89	+229.26
28/10	Piece of History W2.7, Firelight	+0.62	+222.37
27/10	**Sir Psycho W2.54**	+1.46	+221.75
26/10	Aptly Put, Prince Rock	-2	+220.29
25/10	Ice Lord, Camacho Man	-2	+222.29
24/10	**Duke Debarry W7.22,** Daysaq, Almahha	+3.91	+224.29
23/10	Milesha	-1	+220.38

TOP JOCKEY

22/10	Lady Tati, Phoenix Star, A Hundred Echoes	-3	+221.38
21/10	Vitar	-1	+224.38
20/10	**Windsor Avenue W1.9**, Snapdragon Fire	-0.15	+225.38
19/10	Dark Vision	-1	+225.53
18/10	**Futuristic W3.24**, River Camm, Briardale	+0.13	+226.53
17/10	**The King of May W24.0, Good Reason W5.85**	+26.46	+226.40
16/10	Valentino Sunrise, Atheeb, **Khuzaam W2.1, Dawaaween W3.15**	+1.09	+199.94
15/10	Red Nika	-1	+198.85
14/10	Show Palace, **Red Secret W4.3**	+2.14	+199.85
12/10	**Wakefield W5.53**	+4.30	+197.71
11/10	Orvar, Queen Daenerys	-2	+193.41
10/10	Bacchalot, Well Prepared, Great Image	-3	+195.41
9/10	**Oleg W2.3,** Capitaine, Indian Viceroy	-0.77	+198.41
8/10	NO BETS		
7/10	Molten Lava, Witness Protection, **High Accolade W2.29**	-0.77	+199.18
6/10	Sidi Ismael, Highway Companion	-2	+199.95
5/10	**Neff W23.0,**Gleno, Glasvegas, Poetry	+18.85	+201.95
4/10	Always Amazing	-1	+183.10
3/10	Mickey	-1	+184.10
2/10	Purdey's Gift, Stanford, So Sharp, TeetonPowe	-4	+185.10
1/10	Colouring, Manzo Duro, Addis **AdabaW3.63**	+0.50	+189.10
30/9	Amnaa, Forsee	-2	+188.60
29/9	Satis House, **Astrophysics W5.21**	+3.0	+190.60
28/9	Quiet Favour	-1	+187.60
27/9	Al Ozzdi, **Daahyeh W2.66**	+0.58	+188.60
26/9	Boutonniere, Indra Dawn	-2	+188.02
25/9	End Zone, **Convict W2.68**, Bryn Du	-0.40	+190.02
24/9	**Augustus Caesar W2.12**	+1.06	+190.42
23/9	Midas Girl, Grimsthorpe Castle	-2	+191.42
22/9	NO BETS		
21/9	Aluqair	-1	+193.42
20/9	Moudallal, **Separate W15.65**	-1	+194.42
19/9	**Dubai Icon W2.62**	+1.54	+181.00
18/9	**The Herds Garden W9.89**	+8.45	+179.46
17/9	Battle of Wills, **Universal Order W3.8, Tiger Crusade W2.54**	+3.12	+171.01
16/9	Josie Abbing, Isabella's Girl, **Jack D'OrW1.87, Inflamed W5.23**, Treaty of Dingle, **Motagally W3.58**	+4.27	+167.89
15/9	NO BETS		

TOP JOCKEY

14/9	**Involved W32.0, Band Practice W7.8, Attaiment W3.0**, Mykindofsunshine, **Lethal Lunch W6.18**	+42.02	+163.62
13/9	Katrina, Zwayyan, Indian Raj, Qassada	-4	+121.60
12/9	Indian Viceroy	-1	+125.60
11/9	NO BETS		
10/9	**One Night in Milan W3.29, Winding Row W1.18,** Carry On	+1.35	+126.60
9/9	**Kennocha W15.5,** Long Call, Silverturnstogold	+11.78	+125.25
8/9	Convict	-1	+113.47
7/9	Flaming Marvel, Canton Prince	-2	+114.47
6/9	**Riot W1.96,** Total Comitment	+0.09	+116.57
5/9	**Starfighter W3.91, Belated Breath W2.92,** Navaty, **Lucky Robin W1,95**	+4.48	+116.66
4/9	**Fair Power W2.85, Irene May W3.35**	+3.99	+112.18
3/9	Seinsational, Doune Castle	-2	+108.19
2/9	**Bungee Jump W12.5**	+10.93	+110.19
2/9	Arctic Sea	-1	+99.26
2/9	**Desert Point W2.61**	+2.61	+100.26
2/9	Gennady	-1	+98.73
1/9	**Red Alert W11.0, Urban Highway W5.1,** Witness Protection, Imbucato	+11.40	+99.73
31/8	**Gallic W3.5, X Force W5.47,** Forbidden Lad	+5.62	+88.33
30/8	Urban Hero, Fast and Free, **Lyndon B W3.35**	+0.23	+82.71
29/8	**Endless Joy W4.48**	+3.31	+82.48
29/8	**Armandihan W4.3**	+3.14	+79.17
28/8	**Run Wild W7.88**	+6.54	+76.03
28/8	Johnny Kidd, Mums Hope	-2	+69.49
28/8	**Let's Go Lucky W3.6, ChilChil W4.72**	+6.00	+71.49
27/8	**World Title W2.4**	+1.33	+65.49
26/8	**Mega Double W1.98**	+0.93	+64.16
25/8	Royal Welcome, **Bless Him W4.2,** Momkin, **Queens Soldier W2.29. Le Don De Vie W3.3**	+4.45	+63.23
24/8	NO BETS		
23/8	**Cambric W2.06**	+1.01	+58.78
22/8	NO BETS		
21/8	**Indian Viceroy W3.95**	+2.80	+57.77
20/8	Mayne, **Lady Mascara W3.2**	+1.09	+54.97
19/8	**Our Charlie Brown W8.2**	+6.84	+53.88
18/8	NO BETS		
17/8	NO BETS		
16/8	**Laafy W3.7**	+2.57	+47.04
15/8	**Kick on W5.9**	+4.67	+44.47
14/8	**Black Anthem W2.34, Endowed W2.19, Kalsara W4.12**	+5.37	+39.80
13/8	**Kyllang Rock W3.4**	+2.28	+34.43
12/8	NO BETS		
11/8	Maktabba	-1	+32.15
11/8	Restless Rose	-1	+33.15
10/8	**Addeyebb W2.26**	+1.18	+35.15
10/8	**Qaysar W3.35**	+2.23	+33.97
9/8	Mr Dukesbury	-1	+31.74
8/8	River Cam	-1	+32.74
7/8	Indian Viceroy	-1	+33.74
6/8	NO BETS		
5/8	Two Bids, House of Kings, South Coast	-3	+34.74
4/8	NO BETS		
3/8	Buzz, Buriram, Critical Time, **Rose of Kildare DH 6.31**	-0.47	+37.52
2/8	**Rose Hip W2.77**	+1.68	+37.99
1/8	NO BETS		
31/7	**Maamora W5.31**	+4.09	+36.31
30/7	Evita De Musnil, Sudona	-2	+32.22

TOP JOCKEY

Date	Selection		
29/7	Clay Regazzoni	-1	+34.22
29/7	Can't Stop Now	-1	+35.22
28/7	NO BETS		
27/7	Addeybb, Sovereign Duke, Fabulist, Vivid Diamond, Subjectivist	-5	+36.22
27/7	**Global Hunter W1.8**	+0.76	+41.22
26/7	**Path of Thunder W2.56**	+1.48	+40.46
26/7	Turn N Twirl	-1	+38.98
25/7	Unresolved, Lucky Number, Ninjago	-3	+39.98
25/7	**Starczewski W2.42**	+1.35	+42.98
24/7	Reassure	-1	+41.63
23/7	NO BETS		
22/7	**Dubai Future W3.78, Mitty's Smile W3.16,** Boruma, Dagian, Lamloon	+1.69	+42.63
21/7	Capital Force, Ennistown	-2	+40.94
20/7	Frequency Code	-1	+42.94
20/7	**Qutob W4.55, Fred W3.4**	+5.65	+43.94
19/7	National Treasure, **Calculation W2.31**	+0.24	+38.53
19/7	**Salem Zayed W3.25, Corinthian Knight W6.71**	+7.56	+38.29
18/7	NO BETS		
17/7	**Early Summer W5.4, Distant Chimes W2.73, Hydroplane W2.06**	+6.83	+30.73
17/7	**Zumurud W2.73**	+1.64	+23.90
16/7	**How Bizarre W3.35**	+2.23	+22.26
15/7	**Royal Birth W9.2**	+7.79	+20.03
14/7	**What Will Be W3.3**	+2.19	+12.24
13/7	NO BETS		
12/7	**Spartan Fighter W1.59**	+0.56	+10.05
11/7	**Matchmaker W5.8**	+4.56	+9.49
10/7	Mercenary Rose	-1	+4.93
9/7	Big City, Grace Note	-2	+5.93
8/7	**Volatile Analyst W5.3,** Waterfront, Alnadir	+2.09	+7.93
7/7	NO BETS		
6/7	Magical Wish	-1	+5.84
5/7	Makyon, Dorah, Lost in Time, **Brigand W3.94,** Spargrove	-1.21	+6.84
4/7	High Acclaim, Cape Victory	-2	+8.05
4/7	**Cosatline W10.0**	+8.55	+10.05
3/7	Soto Sizzler, **Related W6.52, Gazihave W2.32,** Innocent Touch	+4.50	+1.50
2/7	Fresh New Dawn	-3	-3
1/7	In Trutina, Just That Lord	-2	-2

Printed in Great Britain
by Amazon